WHAT OTHERS ARE SAYING

"Whether it has been snowboarding the slopes of Oregon or Utah, flying a single engine plane across the country or having a cup of coffee, the conversation with Dr. Dan always ends up in the Word of God.

On The Road to Emmaus mines the nuggets of God's Word and reveals the person of Jesus from start to finish.

This is a must-read for any student of scripture who wants to understand what the Old Testament is really all about.

Highly readable, colorfully painted, clearly presented."

—Jim Wright
Lead Pastor of Mountain Church, Medford, Oregon
Author of *Shipwrecks* and *Storm Clouds*

ON THE ROAD TO
EMMAUS

By God's Grace,

[signature]

ON THE ROAD TO
EMMAUS

SEEING JESUS IN THE OLD TESTAMENT

DANIEL TOMLINSON, M.D.

TATE PUBLISHING
AND ENTERPRISES, LLC

Published by Tate Publishing & Enterprises, LLC
127 E. Trade Center Terrace | Mustang, Oklahoma 73064 USA
1.888.361.9473 | www.tatepublishing.com

Tate Publishing is committed to excellence in the publishing industry. The company reflects the philosophy established by the founders, based on Psalm 68:11,
"The Lord gave the word and great was the company of those who published it."

Book design copyright © 2014 by Tate Publishing, LLC. All rights reserved.
Cover design by Ivan Charlem Igot
Interior design by Jimmy Sevilleno

Published in the United States of America
ISBN: 978-1-63268-209-3
Religion / Biblical Criticism & Interpretation / Old Testament
14.05.26

CONTENTS

And he began again to teach by the seaside: And there were gathered unto him a great multitude, so that he entered into a ship, and sat in the sea; and the whole multitude was by the sea on the land. And he taught them many things by parables, and he said unto them in his doctrine, *Hearken:* Behold, there went out a sower to sow: And it came to pass, as he sowed, some fell by the wayside, and the fowls of the air came and devoured it up. And some fell on stony ground, where it had not much earth; and immediately it sprang up, because it had no depth of earth: But when the sun was up, it was scorched; and because it had no root, it withered away. And some fell among thorns, and the thorns grew up, and choked it, and it yielded no fruit. And other fell on good ground, and did yield fruit that sprang up and increased; and brought forth, some thirty, and some sixty, and some an hundred. And he said unto them, *He that hath ears to hear, let him hear* (emphasis mine).

Mark 4:1–9

PREFACE

"THE OLD TESTAMENT is one big picture book!"
That's what the preacher said!

He continued, "You see, we are all children, and we need stories. Like a comic book, we need illustrations in order to learn what our Father would want us to know."

The year was 1995. I had been a Christian for over twenty years, but I had never heard that! You mean the Old Testament isn't just a long treatise on how God wants us to live? How we should try to be good. You mean it's not just the documentation of how we are all inadequate and, thus, need the New Testament with Jesus and his death and resurrection, replacing our inability to save us on our own?

Nope. He said that the Old Testament is the New Testament concealed, and the New Testament is the Old Testament revealed. He continued that the Old Testament stories and pictures typified New Testament principles and truths. Physical battles in the Old portray spiritual battles in the New. For instance, killing every person of an enemy country always sounded pretty harsh to me, but it was really there as an example of the spiritual need to give everything to & for God, whether that be sending the flesh away or following Jesus wholeheartedly. It was talking about the spiritual, not the physical. Applications to my life just started pouring forth. What a revelation it was!

And not only principles but prophecy too. I learned that kings and nations, psalms, and inanimate objects spoke of future events and people. Pictures of Antichrist, Satan, the end times and of course our hero, Jesus Christ, were all there to be amazed by and considered.

So this is the purpose I have and what I want you to experience in writing this book. I hope you get to feel the excitement I felt as you see the Old Testament in a new and bigger way—one big children's book showing us our wonderful Savior Jesus Christ.

INTRODUCTION

Mentioned only one time in all of scripture, one might conclude the little village of Emmaus not to be important in Israel. But nothing could be further from the truth because on resurrection Sunday, the greatest Bible study of all time took place on the road to Emmaus.

> And, behold, two of them went that same day to a village called Emmaus, which was from Jerusalem about (seven miles). And they talked together of all these things which had happened. And it came to pass, that, while they communed together and reasoned, Jesus himself drew near, and went with them. But their eyes were (dulled) that they should not know him. And he said unto them, What manner of communications are these that ye have one to another, as ye walk, and are sad? And the one of them, whose name was Cleopas, answering said unto him, Art thou only a stranger in Jerusalem, and hast not known the things which are come to pass there in these days?

And he said unto them, What things? And they said unto him, Concerning Jesus of Nazareth, which was a prophet mighty in deed and word before God and all the people: And how the chief priests and our rulers delivered him to be condemned to death, and have crucified him. But we trusted that it had been he which should have redeemed Israel: And beside all this, today is the third day since these things were done. Yea, and certain women also of our company made us astonished, which were early at the sepulchre; and when they found not his body, they came, saying, that they had also seen a vision of angels, which said that he was alive. And certain of them which were with us went to the sepulchre, and found it even so as the women had said: But him they saw not. Then he said unto them, O fools, and slow of heart to believe all that the prophets have spoken: Ought not Christ to have suffered these things, and to enter into his glory? [And beginning at Moses (the five books of Moses) and the prophets (prophetical writings), he expounded unto them in all the scriptures the things concerning himself].

Luke 24:13–27

What a Bible study that must have been! Jesus the Christ explained to these two privileged men from *all* the scriptures in the Old Testament speaking of and picturing him. The teacher undoubtedly spoke of Abel, of Joseph, of David, and of Isaac. He must have mentioned Boaz and Joshua and Solomon and Esther. He likely told of how the Old Testament sacrifices, the rock in the wilderness, the tabernacle and the weekly Sabbath all pointed to him. I'm sure he suggested the prophecies of his suffering found in the Psalms, in Isaiah, in Hosea, and in Zechariah. Yes, what a mind-blowing, mind-expanding time that must have been for those two men! Yet, as we read on in this account, we learn that they did not recognize Jesus for who he was until they had broken bread with him.

They said,

> Did not our hearts burn within us, while he talked with us
> by the way, and while he opened to us the scriptures?
>
> Luke 24:32

Their hearts were lit on fire by the words he spoke, yet they recognized him in the breaking of bread. That's still the way it is in our day. The word of God is a lion that when let out of it's cage is powerful and mighty, yet it's when we commune with our Lord when we remember what he did for us at the cross as we take communion that we really see him as the Risen Lord!

Well, after that evening meal with their Lord, the two men rose up and traveled the seven miles back to Jerusalem. This news was just too good to sit on until morning! They found the eleven disciples gathered together and told them, "What things were done in the way, and how he was known of them in breaking of bread" (Luke 24:35).

As they spoke, Jesus himself stood in the midst of them and pronounced, "Shalom (peace)." He then said,

> These are the words which I spake unto you, while I was yet
> with you, that all things must be fulfilled, which were writ-
> ten in the Law of Moses, and in the prophets, and in the
> psalms concerning me. Then opened he their understand-
> ing, that they might understand the scriptures. And said
> unto them, Thus it is written, and thus it behooved Christ
> to suffer, and to rise from the dead the third day: And that
> repentance and remission of sins should be preached in his
> name among all nations, beginning at Jerusalem.
>
> Luke 24:44–47

Now the secret was out! The Old Testament is all about Jesus. If we will look, we will see that the words of Moses and David, the words of Isaiah and Zechariah, all point to him! What a revelation that must have been. What a revelation it still is! Christians, brothers and sisters, the Old Testament is about Jesus! It's not about rules and regulations so much, it's not about Jewish history and poetry per say. It's speaks, it pictures, it typifies our Lord. It tells of our savior and friend in a way that makes it impossible for the man or the woman with eyes to see, to think, and to say anything other than "Jesus is Lord!"

Scholars call this idea of Jesus being interlaced everywhere in the Old Testament the "Red Thread." This is a reference from the story of the time the walls of Jericho came tumbling down. Rahab, a woman who believed in and feared the God of Israel was told that to be saved from the upcoming destruction of the city she would need to hang a red cord out of her window. This was the signal to the men of Israel to spare all who abode in her house on the day they utterly destroyed Jericho. The Red Thread was the mark of her allegiance to Israel just as Jesus, the Red Thread of the Old Testament, is the mark of our allegiance, of our pardon by the Father!

Paul, in his Epistle to the Colossians, stated that the Old Testament words concerning the meat sacrifices, the feast days, and the Sabbath were a shadow of things to come. He too continued to strongly make the connection in his writings between the Old Testament scriptures and their link to the Lord. He wrote to the believers in 1 Corinthians 10, and by extension, to us, that we are not to be ignorant of biblical typology. We are not to be blind to the fact that the Old Testament pictures Jesus and New Testament principles. He made the association that the Jews were baptized in the Red Sea just as we in the New Testament are baptized in the name of the Lord. He said that the rock, which followed them and released water, was Christ, the rock of our salvation.

Yes, Jesus is present everywhere in the Old Testament.

Let's look together. In so doing, we will see people pointing to Jesus, pictures typifying Jesus, prophecies proclaiming Jesus, and poems singing of Jesus.

PART 1

PEOPLE POINTING TO JESUS

ADAM: THE FIRST SPIRITUAL MAN

T HE FIRST MAN, Adam, was our champion. He was a spiritual man who was accustomed to walking with God in the cool of the day. His story is found in the very first chapter of the first book in the Bible. Thus, it is likely that when Jesus began sharing to the two men on the road to Emmaus of the pictures of him in the Old Testament, he may have begun with Adam. Indeed, our main text for this book states, "And beginning at Moses and all the prophets, he expounded unto them in all the scriptures the things concerning himself" (Luke 24:27). Since Adam was a sinless perfect man until he fell, it bears to reason that Adam may have been mentioned initially since he is the first major character whose story is given to us in Moses's writings.

Moreover, Paul adds to this line of reasoning as he comes out and states in the epistle to the Romans that Adam was a picture of our Lord. "Nevertheless death reigned from Adam to Moses, even over them that had not sinned after the similitude of Adam's transgression, *who is the figure of him that was to come*" (Romans 5:14) (emphasis mine). He also stated that Jesus is the last Adam.

> And so it is written, The first man Adam was made a living soul; the last Adam was made a quickening spirit. Howbeit that was not first which is spiritual, but that which is natural; and afterward that which is spiritual. The first man is of the earth, earthy: The second man is the Lord from heaven. As is the earthy, such are they also that are earthy [all of Adam's descendants]: And as is the heavenly, such are they also that are heavenly. And as we have borne the image of the earthy, we shall also bear the image of the heavenly.
>
> 1 Corinthians 15:45–49

Let's look a bit at Adam's story to see the connection.

> And God said, Let us make man in our image, after our likeness: And let them have dominion over the fish of the sea, and over the foul of the air, and over the cattle, and over all the earth, and over every creeping thing that creepeth upon the earth. So God created man in his own image, in the image of God created he him.
>
> Genesis 1:26–27

Adam, that first man, was created in the image of God! We know that "God is Spirit" (John 4:24), and that's how special Adam was. He was a spiritual man. He was complete. Indeed, he was a perfect man who was created to live and fellowship with God on into eternity. If only he could have remained sinless. The one stipulation God placed upon that first man was that he was not to eat of the tree of the knowledge of good and evil. Adam, that spiritual man, was to depend upon his spiritual connection with God over dependence upon the five senses to ascertain knowledge. God stated, "For in the day that thou eatest thereof thou shalt surely die" (Genesis 2:17). Adam knew this full well yet chose to rebel and eat of the fruit of the tree after the love of his life, his darling, had eaten. Paul tells us that Adam was not fooled by Satan. "For Adam was first formed, then Eve. And Adam was not deceived, but the woman being deceived was (1 Timothy 2:13–14). Adam actively chose to disobey God's command not to eat of the fruit of the tree after he learned that Eve had already done so. Why did he do this? He knew he would die!

The reason Adam chose to die is what makes our father Adam a picture of Christ. Adam loved his bride, and now, his bride was "enlightened" if you will. She was tricked into living in the flesh instead of walking by the Spirit. She was now going to die, and Adam knew he would lose her. Adam, in a pathetic attempt to keep his bride, rebelled against God's command and sacrificed his own life by choosing to be with her instead of relying upon God to work out a solution. Adam died for his bride just like the Savior died for his! Jesus, the last Adam, left heaven where he fellowshipped with the Father of lights and became a man of body and soul. Then he died for our sins to rescue us, his bride, back from the clutches of Satan to be with him! Jesus found the love of his life and died for us just as Adam willingly died for his! Truly, Jesus is our champion!

The application to this story is huge. Since Christ has rescued you and me, his bride, back to him, we too now can walk in the Spirit. Or, like our earthly mother and father, we can be tricked into living in the flesh as was Eve, or we can be rebellious and follow after our flesh as did Adam. Unfortunately, walking and living in the flesh still brings death just as it did in the day of Adam and Eve.

Paul states this oh so well.

> For to be carnally minded is death; but to be spiritually minded is life and peace. Because the carnal mind is enmity against God: For it is not subject to the law of God, neither indeed can be. So then, they that are in the flesh cannot please God.
>
> Romans 8:6–8

Walking in the five senses, walking in the flesh cannot please God. The book of Hebrews states this concept with these words, "But without *faith* it is impossible to please him" (Hebrews 11:6) (emphasis mine). Walking in the Spirit, pleasing God, takes faith! Thus, if I want to please God, I must stop listening to what my eyes and ears and feelings tell me and learn to trust what my heart is speaking. Learn to listen to that small still voice that whispers words of wisdom and words of knowledge and discernment of spirits to me (1 Corinthians 12:8–10). I must learn to exercise the gifts of encouragement and giving and teaching and mercy that he gives to me (Romans 12:7–8). So do you!

Oh, one more thing. What's the evidence that I am spirit filled? Why it's how I love! Chapter 13, the love chapter, is sandwiched between chapters 12 and 14 of 1 Corinthians, where the manifestations of the Spirit are discussed. Jesus said, By this shall all men know that ye are my disciples, if you have love one to another (John 13:35).

Lord, help us to walk in the spirit!

For further study:

1. What does walking in the spirit look like compared to walking in the flesh?

2. Can you think of a time when by faith you followed what you believed God was telling you even though your five senses argued against that thought?

3. Why is loving God & people so lovely?

ABEL: THE FIRST
SHEPHERD

ABEL, WHO WAS the second son of Adam and Eve, was given a name that implied Eve's disappointment. She called him "morning mist" or "vanity!" You see. Cain, Eve's first child, was named "gotten," for that mother of us all felt that Cain was the promised one.

> And I will put enmity between thee and the woman, and between thy seed and her seed; it [he] shall bruise thy head, and thou shall bruise his heel.
>
> Genesis 3:15

In naming Cain, she said, "I have gotten a man from the Lord" (Genesis 4:1). Or more properly, "I have gotten *the* man from the Lord."

Soon though, she must have realized that Cain wasn't the man. As Eve saw Cain grow and mature, it became obvious that her little son had inherited the same sin nature of his father Adam. Thus, in naming Abel, Eve pronounced her frustration in not understanding God's promise to her as given earlier in the garden before she and Adam were cast out.

Now, the Bible reveals to us that Abel was a keeper of sheep while Cain was a tiller of the ground. That is, Abel was a shepherd, and Cain was a farmer. On the surface, the significance of this distinction can easily be missed. You see, Abel tended and cared for the gifts God had provided while Cain *worked* for his produce. This is the second picture in the Bible of man working versus accepting God's covering provision. The first example came only a few verses earlier.

> And the eyes of them both were opened, and they knew that they were naked: and they *sewed* fig leaves together, and made themselves aprons (emphasis mine).
>
> Genesis 3:7

And,

> Unto Adam also and to his wife did the Lord God make coats of skins, and clothed them [the skins were likely lamb skins].
>
> Genesis 3:21

You see, God is showing in these very first stories that he is serious about salvation by faith and not by works.

> And in the process of time it came to pass, that Cain brought of the fruit of the ground an offering unto the Lord. And Abel, he also brought of the firstlings of his flock and of the fat thereof. And the Lord had respect unto Abel and his offering: But unto Cain and to his offering he had not respect.
>
> Genesis 4:3–5

God had respect unto Abel's offering because it was of faith and not of works.

> For by grace are ye saved through faith; and not of yourselves: It is the gift of God: Not of works, lest any man should boast.
>
> Ephesians 2:8–9

The book of Hebrews fills in the rest of the details.

> By *faith* Abel offered unto God a more excellent sacrifice than Cain, by which he obtained witness that he was righteous, God testifying of his gifts: And by it he being dead yet speaketh (emphasis mine).
>
> Hebrews 11:4

By comparing scripture with scripture, it becomes clear that God must have told the two boys what to offer, for we learn in Romans of how we obtain faith, "So then faith cometh by hearing, and hearing by the word of God" (Romans 10:17). Nonetheless, Cain did his own thing and worked up an offering, while Abel sacrificed a lamb. Of course Abel's sacrifice is the picture that the Almighty wants us to see. Again and again in the Old Testament, God told his children that a lamb was needed. This culminated in the giving of Jesus, the Lamb of God!

Abel obeyed God and did no work, but instead, he *sacrificed* something dear to him. That's what God was looking for. That's what he is still looking for today from you and me.

Next, the Bible tells that Cain's countenance fell when he learned that his work was nothing but vanity. We would say that he became depressed!

As an aside, this still happens to men today as they come to the end of their lives and see that all of their work is nothing but a vapor! "Again, I considered all travail, and every right work, that for this a man is envied of his neighbor. This is also vanity and vexation of spirit" (Ecclesiastes 4:4).

Cain, in his depression, evidently became angry, bitter, and resentful. Thus, we learn later when the boys were in the field "That Cain rose up against Abel his brother, and slew him (Genesis 4:8). How sad! It took only one chapter in the Bible for man to progress from rebellion to outright murder! Truly, sin brings nothing but death!

This first murder brought immediate judgment from the Lord. God said, "The voice of thy brother's blood crieth unto me from the ground" (Genesis 4:10). More properly, the word for blood is plural—bloods. God was saying that all of those who would follow from Abel will now never be born! It was their blood, all of those unborn, who cried to God. And they cried for judgment! As I consider this verse, I fear for our nation. America, the land of Roe verses Wade, continues to say it is fine to kill unborn people! I can't help but think that the voices of their bloods also rise up crying for judgment!

Okay, that's Abel's story. Abel, the second son of Eve, the boy with the name of morning mist was a powerful picture of Jesus Christ and, undoubtedly, was included in our Lord's words to the two men on the road to Emmaus. It's easy now to see why. Abel was the first shepherd just as the Bible tells us that Jesus is the good, the great and the chief shepherd! (John 10:14, Hebrews 13:20, 1 Peter 5:4) Abel offered a blood sacrifice that was respected by the Father just as Jesus *became* the blood sacrifice. Abel offered a lamb, just as Jesus *became* the Lamb. As John the Baptist so pogointly stated, "Behold, the Lamb of God, which taketh away the sin of the world" (John 1:29). Abel was killed by his brother just as Yeshua, Jesus, was killed by his brothers—the Jews. Abel's blood cried out for judgment, and likewise, Jesus' blood cries out. But in his case, not for judgment but for forgiveness!

> And to Jesus, the mediator of the new covenant, and to the blood of sprinkling, that speaketh better things than that of Abel.
>
> Hebrews 12:24

Abel, not Eve's first son, but her second, was a man from the Lord! Eve had come full circle. In Cain, she believed she had received "the man from the Lord," but he was only "a morning mist." But in Abel, the one she called "morning mist," the one who proclaimed her disappointment, he was really the one who pictured powerfully "the man from the Lord!"

Before moving on to another Old Testament picture of Jesus Christ, an important application to my life needs to be considered. The Bible states that Cain's countenance fell after he realized that his works were of no value to the Lord. He became depressed. Then over the process of time, we learned that while they were in the field that Cain "Rose up against Abel his brother, and slew him" (Genesis 4:8). How does that happen? How does a man fall into what Jude calls "The way of Cain" (Jude 11)? How does a person go from being depressed to becoming angry, bitter, jealous, and envious enough to fall into a murderous rage?

Well, you know the word of God will give us that answer. It's a two-fold answer we must keep in our hearts as we all are challenged in this world to become bitter and angry.

> For this is the message that ye heard from the beginning, that we should *love* one another. Not as Cain, who was of that wicked one, and slew his brother. And wherefore slew he him? Because his own *works* were evil, and his brother's righteous. (emphasis mine)
>
> 1 John 3:11–12

Once again we learn that Cain's works were evil in God's economy, while his brother's sacrifice was not. But look at the new information. In his anger and bitterness, Cain evidently opened himself up to devil possession. The Bible states that he was "of that wicked one!" I don't want to go there after thinking about this story! If I let anger and bitterness reign, over time, it will open the door to Satan and his henchmen to come in and ruin me!

The antidote that John gives? Why love, of course!

From the beginning, from this very early story in the Bible, we can see that love is the key. Love is the force that will hold back my evil heart from being taken down that road of bitterness.

Here's other important words to consider.

> Let all bitterness, and wrath, and anger, and clamor, and evil speaking, be put away from you, with all malice: And be ye kind one to another, tenderhearted, *forgiving* one another, even as God for Christ's sake hath forgiven you (emphasis mine).
>
> Ephesians 4:31–32

Forgiveness! The antidote for the bitterness, wrath, and anger that can so easily well up in me is to forgive.

Well, you say that's not so easy; you don't know what he did to me! You don't know my story. I can't do that! You're right; I don't know *your* story, but I know *his* story! Jesus took my sins, yours too, and went to the cross to redeem us back to the Father. When I contemplate on what he did for me, how God for Christ's sake has forgiven me, then and only then can I forgive that person where otherwise I would be unable. Then and only then can I let go of the bitterness and anger that would otherwise lead me into "the way of Cain!"

Two important words, two important concepts that I must constantly consider are love and forgiveness. Forgiveness and love are keys to the abundant life in Jesus Christ!

For further study:

1. Why is the doctrine of salvation by works such an insult to Jesus and his work on the cross?

2. What factors come to bear to make something I offer to God a true sacrifice?

3. Do you find it sometimes hard to forgive someone who has wronged you? How can our Lord's sacrifice for our sins help you to forgive that person who has done something unforgivable?

MELCHIZEDEK: THE KING AND PRIEST

MELCHIZEDEK, WHOSE NAME means "king of righteousness" was both a king and a priest. He perfectly reveals Jesus Christ as we shall see. He undoubtedly was part of the explanation that our Lord gave to those two blessed men on the road to Emmaus.

We are first introduced to Melchizedek in Genesis 14. In that chapter, we find the first mention of war in the Bible. Four kings and their servants took on five kings in the area of the lower Jordan River Valley, the vicinity of what we know of today as the Dead Sea. In this region, the ancient cities of Sodom and Gomorrah where located, and it was there that Abraham's nephew Lot resided. Lot and all that he owned was taken as spoil by Chedorlaomer the victor. They were taken far to the north, to the border of present day Lebanon and Syria. The taking of Lot enraged Abraham. Thus, the man the Bible calls "the father of faith" armed his many servants, and at great risk to himself and his family took on Chedorlaomer and rescued Lot along with all of his possessions. It was a nighttime raid, probably somewhat stealthful, so on the way back, Abraham was likely in a hurry to get back to the safety of his land. It was there that he met Melchizedek.

> And Melchizedek King of Salem brought forth bread and wine: And he was priest of the most high God. And he blessed him, and said, Blessed by Abram of the most high God, possessor of heaven and earth.
>
> Genesis 14:18–19

It's pretty easy to see Jesus in this story, isn't it! We have Melchizedek, whose name means king of righteousness and whose position is as king of Salem. In English, that means king of peace. We might equate this to Jesus's title as the prince of peace. Also, Salem is likely an early title for the City of the Great King, i.e. Jerusalem!

This king, who also is a priest, offered to Abraham bread and wine. These of course are pictures of our Lord's body and blood. These gifts typify what Jesus did for Abraham and, by extension, for all of his children in sacrificing his perfect body and blood to save us.

The book of Hebrews chimes in with more information linking Melchizedek to Jesus.

> For this Melchisedec, King of Salem, priest of the most high God, who met Abraham returning from the slaughter of the kings, and blessed him...first being by interpretation King of Righteousness, and after that also King of Salem, which is, King of Peace; Without father, without mother, without descent, having neither beginning of days, nor end of life; but made like unto the Son of God; abideth a priest continually.
>
> Hebrews 7:1–3

Without father or mother? Without beginning or end of life? This doesn't sound too ordinary! This sounds like Melchizedek is Jesus himself! Many Bible scholars believe just that. That is, Melchizedek not only pictures Jesus's kingly and priestly ministry, but he *is* Jesus in a pre-incarnate form before Jesus came as the babe of Bethlehem. The biblical term for this is called a *Christophany*. There are other examples of Jesus appearing in the Old Testament, which you can study on your own if you desire. I'll give you a couple to think about. Look at the times the words *the angel of the Lord* appears in the Old Testament. Many times, that majestic angel is treated as deity and accepts worship as no angel would. Secondly, as General Joshua was preparing to take Jericho, he encountered *the captain of the host of the Lord*. This mighty figure also accepted Joshua's worship. Again, this warrior was a Christophany.

Thus, Abraham was wonderfully blessed by the appearance of Melchizedek. Let's look at a few other Bible passages that our Lord would have included in his explanation of the tie between Melchizedek and himself from the scriptures on the road to Emmaus.

> The Lord hath sworn, and will not repent, Thou art a priest forever after the order of Melchizedek.
>
> Psalm 110:4

It is common knowledge to Jews of all times that Psalm 110 is a prophetic psalm detailing the glorious ministry of the coming messiah. Jesus himself quoted from this Psalm in speaking of himself when he baffled the scribes and Pharisees as they were attempting to trick him during his fateful last week of ministry (Matthew 22:44). In this psalm, the Father is talking to the Son and proclaiming to us of the Son's role in the affairs of men. We are told that Jesus is waiting until the Father makes his enemies his footstool (verse 1); that Jesus will rule in strength from Zion (*Jerusalem.* verse 2); that all will love and adore him in the day of his glory (verse 3); and that Jesus is a new type of priest, one after the order of Melchizedek and not after the order of Aaron (verse 4).

You see, Aaron was of the tribe of Levi and the brother of Moses. In establishing the first priesthood, God chose the Levites. In establishing the kingly line, God chose Judah. He told Jacob that the scepter would come from Judah (Genesis 49:10), but here in Psalm 110, God is revealing that their will be a second priesthood, one that is completely separate from the first. We know this needed to be the case. For Jesus is the mediator of a new covenant (Hebrews 8:6). In Jesus, we are no longer under the law of Moses but now are under the covenant of grace.

Melchizedek was a king and a priest. But no Levitical priest could serve as king. Likewise, no king could serve as a priest after the order of Aaron. In Israel's history, whenever a king tried to serve in the function as a priest, bad things happened.

Remember when Saul sacrificed to God instead of waiting on Samuel. That disobedience lead to his downfall (1 Samuel 13:12–13). Later, when King Uzziah offered incense upon the altar of the Lord, he was struck with leprosy (2 Chronicles 26:16). These men were blurring the picture God was projecting, that is, no person of the children of Israel is qualified to serve as king and priest except the Son, except the Messiah, except our Lord. Indeed, Jesus is the only one who is after the order of Melchizedek!

Continuing, the author of the book of Hebrews asks the following important question.

> If therefore perfection were by the Levitical priesthood [for under it the people received the law], what further need was there that another priest should rise after the order of Melchisedec, and not be called after the order of Aaron?
>
> Hebrews 7:11

Paul stated the same thing when he said that the law (including the Levitical priesthood) was our schoolmaster until Christ

(Galatians 3:24). We would say in the language of today that is impossible to completely follow the Law, thus it is impossible for the Law to make us perfect!

> For the priesthood being changed, there is made of necessity a change also of the law. For he whom these things are spoken pertaineth to another tribe, of which no man gave attendance at the altar. For it is evident that our Lord sprang out of Judah; of which tribe Moses spake nothing concerning priesthood. And it is yet far more evident: For that after the similitude of Melchisedec there ariseth another priest, who is made, not after the law of a carnal commandment, but after the power of an endless life. For he testifieth, Thou art a priest forever after the order of Melchisedec. For there is a verily a disannulling of the commandment going before for the weakness and unprofitable-ness thereof. For the law made nothing perfect, but the bringing in of a better hope did; by the which we draw nigh unto God.
>
> Hebrews 7:12–19

Because the law was weak and unprofitable, not able to make us perfect, our high priest could not come from the priesthood it included. The priest could not come from Aaron. But coming from King Melchizedek, we have a priest who has the power of an endless life, one who brings in a better hope, one in which we can draw near to God!

> By so much was Jesus made a surety [guarantee] of a better testament [covenant]. And they truly were many priests, because they were not suffered to continue by reason of death.
>
> Hebrews 7:22–23

The writer of Hebrews is stating the obvious! You know this is true because all other priests have died!

But this man, because he continues forever, hath an unchangeable priesthood. Wherefore he is able to save to the uttermost all that come unto God by him, seeing he ever liveth to make intercession for them.

Hebrews 7:24–25

Jesus is able to save to the uttermost! He is able to save in all categories of life. Because, like Melchizedek, he lives forever and ever continues to intercede for us. What a wonderful Savior we have! What a great high priest he is!

Now, before we leave the story of the kingly priest Melchizedek, we should think what these things mean to our lives today. Because Jesus, the high priest, offered the bread and wine of his perfect body and blood, we are set free from our sins, not just from year to year as were they under that first priesthood, but we are set free forever! The sacrifice is complete, the sacrifice took. How do I know? Because the Father ratified it by the raising of his Son from the dead! When Jesus stepped out of that tomb, he proved to all that he is the one and only one who can save to the uttermost!

So I want to follow this one who lives forever more. I want to contemplate and meditate about what he was and is about. I don't want to forget that it's all about him! When I do, and that is far too often, my life gets out of kilter. But when I come back to what he has done for me on the cross, how he died for me, how he took my place, then I get back into the proper balance. Then I can take the cares and worries of this life a whole lot less seriously. Then I remember that this life is just the beginning of something that is a whole lot more real, a whole lot more permanent, a whole lot more wonderful!

For further study:

1. Can you think of any other Christophanies in the Old Testament?

2. How does Jesus intercede to the Father on your behalf? Are their any activities or attitudes in which he interceding for you now?

3. Why should the sacrament of communion be important to your Christian life & walk?

ISAAC: THE PROMISED SON'S SACRIFICE

ONE OF THE most profound pictures of Jesus Christ found in the Old Testament is the story of Isaac. You may remember that Isaac was the second son of Abraham as our father of faith had previously sired a son named Ishmael though a union with Hagar, Sarah's Egyptian handmaid. God did not recognize that coming together as Abraham's covenant line and, thus, appeared to him with an unbelievable promise.

Look with me at what the Almighty said,

> And when Abraham was ninety nine years old, the Lord appeared to him and said unto him, I am the Almighty God...I will make my covenant between me and thee, and will multiply thee exceedingly...Thou shalt be a father of many nations...and I will make thee exceedingly fruitful, and I will make nations out of thee, and kings shall come

out of thee. And I will establish my covenant between me and thee and thy seed after thee in their generations for an everlasting covenant, to be a God unto thee, and to thy seed after thee. And God said unto Abraham, As for Sarai thy wife, thou shalt not call her name Sarai, but Sarah shall her name be. And I will bless her and give thee a son of her: Yea, I will bless her, and she shall be a mother of nations; kings and people shall be of her. Then Abraham fell upon his face, and laughed, and said in his heart, Shall a child be born unto him that is a hundred years old? And shall Sarah, that is ninety years old, bear? And God said, Sarah thy wife shall bear thee a son indeed: And thou shalt call his name Isaac: And I will establish my covenant with him for an everlasting covenant, and with his seed after him.

Genesis 17:1–19 (excerpts)

In Isaac, shall thy seed be called! Through Isaac, the boy whose name means "laughter," the boy who was conceived miraculously, would come the everlasting covenant. Likewise Jesus, son of Abraham and Isaac, the completer of the everlasting covenant was also a promised Son who would be conceived supernaturally.

Moreover the Lord spake again unto Ahaz, saying, Ask thee a sign of the Lord thy God: Ask it either in the depth, or in the height above [Go ahead Ahaz, ask for something outrageous in order that I can prove to you who I am!] But Ahaz said, I will not ask, neither will I tempt the Lord. And he said, Hear ye now, O house of David: Is it a small thing for you to weary men, but will ye weary my God also? Therefore the Lord himself shall give you a sign: Behold, a virgin shall conceive, and bear a son, and shall call his name Emmanuel.

Isaiah 7:10–14

As we know from the gospel accounts, the angel Gabriel appeared to a virgin named Mary, and she conceived the Messiah prior to consummating her marriage to her husband Joseph.

Jesus, the Christ, was the outlandish sign, which God, through Isaiah, gave to King Ahaz and to all the house of David!

Continuing with Isaac's depiction of the Lord, we come to wonderful chapter 22 of the book of Genesis.

> And he (God) said, Take now thy son, thine only son Isaac, whom thou lovest, and get thee into the land of Moriah; and offer him there for a burnt offering upon one of the mountains which I will tell thee of.
>
> Genesis 22:2–3

Wait a minute! God told this great man Abraham, this man who had walked with him for decades to do what! Yes, that's right; God did tell Abraham to take the promised son, the one from which would come nations and kings, and to offer him as a sacrifice back to him! Why would Abraham do a crazy thing like that? How could our father of faith actually carry out this command?

The book of Hebrews gives us the answer.

> By faith Abraham, when he was tried, offered up Isaac: And he that had received the promises offered up his only begotten son, of whom it was said [promised], that in Isaac shall thy seed be called: Accounting that God was able to raise him up, even from the dead;
>
> Hebrews 11:17–19

This is great faith! We who live in the twenty-first century know the story. We can see the type. We believe in the resurrection! Abraham didn't have the benefit of knowing Jesus' story. In his day, resurrection wasn't a reality! It wasn't something that people hoped for! Indeed, Abraham truly is the father of faith! He was the author of outrageous faith!

Continuing with these verses, look back at verse 2. God told Abraham to go to the land of Moriah. "Foreseen of the Lord" is the meaning of the word *Moriah* and according to 2 Chronicles 3:1, Mount Moriah is the exact location where Solomon built the temple of the Lord. This is eye opening! The place where sacrifice was later offered up to God for the sins of the people is the place where God told Abraham to sacrifice his son Isaac! We remember in Jesus' story that our Lord was sacrificed outside of the camp on Calvary. Well, the hill we know as Golgotha, the place of the skull, is actually the uppermost portion of Mount Moriah!

I suspect you are starting to see why Isaac certainly was included in the teacher's remarks to those two men on the road to Emmaus. Hang on, there's more!

God also told Abraham in verse 2 that Isaac was to be a burnt offering. We will see later when we come to the "Pictures of Jesus" portion of this book that the burnt offering was a voluntary offering, which pictures the savior's total consecration and dedication in doing the Father's will.

> And Abraham rose up early in the morning...and went to *the place* of which God had told him. (emphasis mine)
>
> Genesis 22:3

> And when they were come to *the place*, which is called Calvary, there they crucified him. (emphasis mine)
>
> Luke 23:33

Again, the place called Moriah and the place called Calvary are one in the same!

> And Abraham took the wood of the burnt offering, and laid it upon Isaac his son: And he took the fire in his hand, and a knife...
>
> Genesis 22:6

These items of course picture Jesus' cross, the fire of God's wrath toward sin and the Roman centurion's spear, which was thrust into the heart of our redeemer!

> And Isaac spake unto Abraham his father and said... Behold the fire and the wood: But where is the lamb for a

burnt offering? And Abraham said, my son, *God will pro-vide himself a lamb for a burnt offering*: (emphasis mine)

Genesis 22:7–8

People read this verse as "Don't worry Isaac, God will provide us a lamb." Sort of like Abraham is holding back on Isaac as to what God told him was needed. But that's not what it says. It doesn't say God will provide us a lamb; it says, God will provide *himself* a lamb! That is, God himself *is* the lamb!

We know this to be true as later John the Baptist said to those gathered at the River Jordan, "Behold the Lamb of God, which taketh away the sins of the world" (John 1:29).

The story climaxed with Abraham and Isaac arriving at Calvary and building the altar of sacrifice. Abraham then bound Isaac and laid him upon the wood. Next, in an eye-closing and chair-gripping moment, Abraham stretched forth his hand, which held the knife, and would have slain his son, when the angel of the Lord called out to him to cease from the sacrifice!

Wow! Abraham was really going to do it! This is incredible to me. I could no more do that than I could swim across Lake Michigan! But somehow, through all of Abraham's past dealings with God, he had come to the place of this kind of incredible faith! Faith that moves mountains! Faith that the raises the dead! Faith that believes God no matter what!

Of course, in staying the sacrifice, this is the only place where the analogy breaks down. For in the greater than Isaac, in Jesus Christ, the Father did not spare his Son. God indeed, did provide himself a lamb. He is the lamb of God who takes away the sins of the world. My sins and your sins taken away!

As an application, I must question what would have happened if Abraham would not have been listening at that moment when God called out from heaven telling him not to offer his son. Well, obviously, Abraham would have killed Isaac! And that's another lesson in this story. Abraham apparently *was* listening. I need to do that too! This story shows me that revelation from God can change. If I'm not listening constantly, then I may get the first part of the message only to miss the second or third part. In fact, in studying God's dealings with men, the author of life hardly ever lets us in on the *big picture*! Ask Job and Jonah to get more amplification on this concept. God prefers to give progressive revelation to you and me to build our faith. It's one step at a time with him.

As an extension of this idea, has God ever asked you to do something painful like he did in our story to Abraham? Have you ever felt convicted to give a painful amount of money as an offering to him or stirred to give up a valued possession or to go and serve in an uncomfortable setting? It may be that God is proving you just like he proved Abraham. It may be that God wants to see if you will actually do the seemingly outrageous thing that he is calling you to do! It's not for him though. He already knows what will happen. It's for you; it's for me! We get to find out, get to pass the test, and get to have a story too!

And the cool part is that when we are victorious, we are blessed far beyond what we were asked to sacrifice. As I give to the Lord, I know that God will be a debtor to no man. I always receive back more than I let go! As I agree to release that possession, often God will say, "Good. Now that you see that you can live without that, why don't you just keep it anyway!" As you serve in an uncomfortable setting, guess what, things start to get comfortable! That's what happened to Abraham.

> Because you have done this thing, and hast not withheld thy son, thine only son...I will bless thee...I will multiply thy seed as the stars of the heaven, and as the sand which is upon the sea shore...and in thy seed shall all the nations of the earth be blessed; because thou hast obeyed my voice.
>
> Genesis 22:16–18

Truly, the repercussions of faith are enormous! Not only affecting the believer himself but blessing generations that follow after!

For further study:

1. Have you ever had your faith tested in a painful way when you were unsure of God's plan?

2. Did God ever wait until the last possible moment to rescue you from a faith testing calamity? Would it have been better or worse for your faith if he had come through sooner?

3. Thinking back on your life. What were the steps God used to lead you to the place you are today? Were there times you wish you would have listened closer?

JOSEPH: BETRAYED
BY HIS BROTHERS

AFTER JESUS EXPLAINED Isaac's story to those two blessed men on the road to Emmaus, he undoubtedly came to Joseph. And what a story he could tell! Remember, Jesus had just been rejected by his brothers, the leaders of Israel. It was the third day after all of these things had transpired, and now the echo of Joseph's rejection could be heard loudly!

Let's listen.

> Joseph was with his brethren and brought unto his father their evil report. Now Israel loved Joseph...And when his brethren saw that their father loved him...they hated him and could not speak peaceably to him. And Joseph dreamed a dream and he told his brethren: And they hated him yet more...And his brethren envied him.
>
> Genesis 37:3–11 (excerpts)

Just as Jesus was not what his brothers, the Jews, expected in the Messiah so too Joseph, as the youngest of his ten brothers in this story, was hated and envied. Jesus spoke the truth to the men of Israel and the truth they could not bear. Likewise, Joseph prophesied hard truths, which also his brothers, the men from which the tribes of Israel were formed, could not accept.

> And Israel said to Joseph, Do not thy brethren feed the flock in Shechem? Go I pray thee, and see if it be well with thy brethren...so he sent him out of the vale of Hebron, and he came to Shechem.
>
> Genesis 37:13–14

Israel, who pictures the Father in this story was concerned about Joseph's brothers. They were in Shechem. The significance of their locale can easily be missed but is an important little nugget. Shechem was the town just outside of the promised land, where Jacob had first resided when had returned from the east. There, his daughter Dianna was raped by the son of the town leader, and Simeon and Levi retaliated by killing the men of Shechem. This place had bad memories for Jacob and rightly so!

So in telling Joseph to seek out his brethren in Shechem, Jacob was really telling him to go get those boys out of that bad place. Likewise, the Father saw the nation of Israel living in a place outside of his promises and called his son Jesus to visit them.

In Joseph's story, we learned that he left his father in Hebron to visit his brothers. Once again, the name of the city tells a story. In this case, *Hebron* means "fellowship!" Joseph left the place of fellowship with his father just as Jesus left heaven, that place of perfect fellowship with the Father, to look for his brethren!

> And he came to Shechem. And a certain man found him, and, behold, he was wondering in the field: And the man asked him, saying, What seekest thou? And he said, I seek my brethren: Tell me, I pray thee, where they feed their flocks. And the man said, they are departed hence; for I

heard them say, Let us go to Dothan. And Joseph went
after his brethren, and found them in Dothan.

Genesis 37:15–17

The men of Israel left the place outside of the promised land
and now were in Dothan. The meaning of Dothan tells of their
state for Dothan means "two wells" or more correctly in this story,
it means "double pits" or "double darkness." The brothers were in
a place of double darkness just as the nation of Israel had been led
into a place outside of God's word and promises by their double
errors of rituals and traditions.

And when they saw him afar off, even before he came near
unto them, they conspired against him to slay him.

Genesis 37:18

Likewise, the Jews also conspired to slay Jesus when he was
still far from them. They saw him as rabble-rousing rabbi from
a no-name village in Galilee. In their preconceived blindness of
who Jesus was and where he came from, they were unable to see
the light of the world!

And they said one to another, Behold, this dreamer
cometh. Come now therefore, and let us slay him, and cast
him into some pit…And Reuben heard it, and delivered
him out of their hands; and said let us not kill him.

Genesis 37:19–21

In like manner, "Then said Pilate to the chief priests and to
the people, I find no fault in this man" (Luke 23:4). Reuben, the
oldest of the brothers and supposedly the leader, like Pilate, was
ultimately inept and unable to save Joseph from the evil inten-
tions of his brothers.

And it came to pass, when Joseph was come to his brethren, that they stripped Joseph out of his coat, his coat of

many colors that was on him; and they took him, and cast him into a pit.

Genesis 37:23–24

Jesus too was stripped, abused, and subsequently cast into the pit we know as the garden tomb.

And they drew and lifted up Joseph out of the pit, and sold Joseph for twenty pieces of silver:

Genesis 37:28

True to the type, Jesus arose out of the tomb also. But instead of twenty pieces of silver, our Lord was betrayed into that pit for thirty pieces (Matthew 26:15)!

In Joseph's story, he left and went to Egypt, where he became second only to pharaoh in power and prestige. For the last two thousand years, Jesus has risen to be with the Father, where he too has been glorified equal to the almighty. In Joseph's story, he later tested his brothers when they came to Egypt to buy bread early in the seven-year worldwide famine. Likewise, Jesus will test his brethren, the Jews, in that still-to-come seven-year famine we understand to be the tribulation. Jesus will subsequently rescue his family just as the one who is pictured in our story rescued Jacob and the sons of Israel in that day.

Yes, most certainly, Joseph's ordeal was included on that wonderful walk on the road to Emmaus!

Before we leave Joseph's amazing testimony, we must again reflect upon the oft repeated truth in God's Word that things are not always as they appear! From Joseph's perspective, his life was a mess. He was abused by his brethren, sold into slavery, and later betrayed by the wife of his master, Potiphar, who had him placed in jail for two years. Things could not have been worse for him really. All the while, Jacob, his father, was led to believe that his beloved son was dead, killed by some wild beast. He was quoted as saying, "For I will go down into the grave unto my son mourning" (Genesis 37:35). And, "Me have ye bereaved of my children: Joseph is not, and Simeon is not, and ye will take Benjamin away: All these things are against me" (Genesis 42:36).

Neither Joseph nor Jacob understood that God was behind the scenes working everything out to fulfill the bigger purpose. To complete the *big idea*! In this case, God used Joseph to deliver his brothers from their pathetic and starved state just as Jesus was used to deliver both Jew and Gentile from our hopeless and doomed condition.

Later, Joseph did receive insight into the reasons for his plight. He said to his brothers,

> Now therefore be not grieved, nor angry with yourselves, that ye sold me hither: For God did send me before you to preserve life. ...And God sent me before you to preserve you a posterity in the earth, and to save your lives by a great deliverance.
>
> Genesis 45:5 and 7

On that day still to come, we will hear the angel say "Even so, Lord God Almighty, true and righteous are thy judgments" (Revelation 16:7).

Yes, God's ways are not our ways. God plans are not always how we might map things out. And most importantly, God does not exist for us! On the contrary, we exist for him. He is the potter, and we are the clay. His purposes will always be achieved. And wonderfully, we must always remember when we come to that place of uncertain grief and pain that God is in control, that God is on the throne, that God has the whole world in his hand!

> And we know that all things work together for good to them that love God, to them who are called according to his purpose.
>
> Romans 8:28

For further study:

1. Have you even been betrayed by a brother or a close friend? How do you believe Jesus felt when he was betrayed?

2. How has life's appearances been deceiving to you? Can you think of a time when circumstances looked bad but ultimately turned out good?

3. Joseph told his brothers "ye thought evil against me; but God meant it unto good" Genesis 50:20). Has anyone ever dealt in an evil manner toward you but God turned it to good?

BENJAMIN: SON OF MY RIGHT ARM

I N THE YOUNGEST son of Jacob, we have yet another picture of Jesus Christ. His name does the painting.

> And they journeyed from Bethel; and there was a little way to come to Ephrath [Bethlehem]: And Rachel travailed, and she had hard labor. And it came to pass, when she was in hard labor, that the midwife said unto her, Fear not; thou shalt have this son also. And it came to pass, as her soul was departing, (for she died) that she called his name Benoni: But his father named him Benjamin.
>
> Genesis 35:16–18

In her sorrow and grief and in her travail and despair as life departed from her, Rachel named her son Benoni. "Son of my sorrow" is the name she gave her son. In her sorrow, in her labor, and in her death, she brought forth life!

That's what Jesus did also. In his sorrow, in his labor, in his death on the cross, he too gave life. Life to you and me, life to all who would come to him! Jesus is Benoni! Jesus is son of my sorrow!

> Behold, my servant...he hath no form or comeliness; and when we shall see him, there is no beauty that we should desire him. He is despised and rejected of men; a man of sorrows and acquainted with grief...Surely he hath borne our griefs, and carried our sorrows...For he was cut off from the land of the living: For the transgression of my people was he stricken.
>
> Isaiah 52 and 53 (excerpts)

And yet Jacob, his father, renamed his son "Benjamin." The new name the patriarch gave his son means "son of my right arm." No longer was Benjamin to be the son who reminded Jacob of the sorrow he and Rachel shared. His son was to be his strength. Benjamin was the *completer* of his posterity. Benjamin was his glory!

Likewise, the Lord Jesus is the *completer*, is the strength, is the glory of his Father. In his sorrow, he too became the Son of his Father's right arm.

> Let this mind be in you, which was also in Christ Jesus: Who, being in the form of God thought it not robbery to be equal with God; but made himself of no reputation, and took upon him the form of a servant, and was made in the likeness of men: And being found in fashion as a man, he humbled himself, and became obedient unto death, even the death of the cross.
>
> Philippians 2:5–8

This is Benoni!

> Wherefore God also hath highly exalted him, and given him a name which is above every name: That at the name

of Jesus every knee should bow, of things in heaven, and things in earth, and things under the earth; And that every tongue should confess that Jesus Christ is Lord, to the glory of God the Father.

Philippians 2:9–11

This is Benjamin! This is the new name that was given to the son of sorrows, the new name that is above every name, the name indicative of his Father's strength and glory.

Now the application to this story is vitally important. Like Rachel, like Jesus, I need to die. In dying, there is life! It's a paradox, yet I know it is true. When I die to myself I actually begin to live. When I stop thinking about myself and look to build up others, then I find life. That's all that dying to self means! Stop thinking about me! Forget about me! Think to bless others, think to sacrificially help others like Jesus did, then I too will be exalted and honored! I too will be given a new name.

Him that overcometh will I make a pillar in the temple of my God, and he shall go no more out: And I will write upon him the name of my God, and the name of the city of my God, which is new Jerusalem, which cometh down out of heaven from my God: And I will write upon him my new name.

Revelation 3:12

For further study:

1. Have you ever labored in sorrow and seen life come in someone else as the result?

2. "In dying one finds life" is a bible paradox. Can you think of any other bible paradoxes in spiritual life?

3. What can you do today to die to self in order to bless another?

MOSES: A PROPHET
LIKE UNTO ME

THE TIES BETWEEN Israel's most revered leader and the Messiah are huge. Certainly Jesus, in his words to the men on the road to Emmaus commented upon the lawgiver Moses! For Moses himself told the Jews that he was a forerunner of the prophet.

> The Lord thy God will raise up unto thee a Prophet from the midst of thee, of thy brethren, like unto me; unto him ye shall hearken...and I will put my words in his mouth; and he shall speak unto them all that I shall command him.
>
> Deuteronomy 18:15 and 18

Let's consider how Jesus may have made the connection in considering their two stories.

First, in their early days, Moses and Jesus had been determined to die, yet they were rescued miraculously. Pharaoh had decreed that all Jewish male newborns were to be executed in the Nile River in order to keep the slave population from becoming too large and hard to control. But when Moses was delivered, his mother hid him for several months. When he became too big to hide, his mother made an ark and placed him in God's providential hands upon that same Egyptian river, where he should have been drowned. Comically, the pharaoh's own daughter rescued Moses and raised him as her own son!

Jesus also had a death sentence upon his head. When Herod learned from the wise men of the east that a great king had been born in Judea, he plotted to kill that future royal before he could rise to glory and power. Herod had his men kill all the male boys less than two years of age who lived in Bethlehem. Only days prior to this travesty, an angel warned Jesus' earthly father, Joseph, that he should flee with his wife and child before the orders of King Herod could be carried forth.

Next, Moses rose to second in all of Egypt, yet according to Hebrews 11, he chose to be with the people of God and to suffer the reproaches of Christ over the treasures of Egypt. Likewise, Jesus as the second person of the trinity willingly chose to leave heaven to rescue the people of God and to be the reproached Christ.

Both Moses and Jesus were rejected by the Jews. In Acts 7, we are told that Moses at the age of forty presented himself to his brethren after delivering one of their own out of the clutches of an Egyptian taskmaster. Thinking that they would understand how God by his hand would deliver them, he was shocked to hear them say, "Who made thee a ruler and a judge over us" (Acts 7:27)? So too, the men of Judah also said of Emmanuel throughout the three year time of "God with us" that they would not have him rule over them!

Oh, there are so many more similarities. Time does not allow me to develop them in detail. But I must list them for you as I feel our Lord did for those men on that day nearly two thousand years ago.

The Bible states Moses was the meekest man upon the face of the earth (Numbers 12:3). Jesus, in his only autobiographical statement of himself, said that he is meek and lowly in heart (Matthew 11:29).

On numerous occasions, Moses interceded for the people. Likewise, the Word tells us that Jesus is sitting at God's right hand, interceding on our behalf.

Moses's face glowed after he returned from God's presence. In like manner, our Lord's face appeared as the sun when he was transfigured on Mount Hermon.

God appointed Moses to deliver his children from the bondage of Egypt. God appointed Jesus to deliver his children from the bondage of sin!

Moses was the giver of the law. Jesus was the deliverer who freed us from our inability to keep the law!

Moses instituted the Passover sacrifice (Hebrews 11:28). Jesus was the Passover sacrifice (1 Corinthians 5:7).

Moses, a Jewish man, married a Gentile bride named Zipporah. Christ, also a Jewish man, calls the church, made up of Jews and Gentiles, his bride.

Moses was a shepherd for his father-in-law, Jethro. Jesus is the shepherd who seeks the lost sheep of his Father, God.

Moses's hand became leprous then was restored. Jesus became leprous (he became sin for us) then was restored (resurrected)!

Moses lifted up the serpent in the wilderness, and the people lived. Jesus told Nicodemus that he too would be lifted up, as that serpent was, so the people will live.

Moses parted the Red Sea; Jesus calmed the Galilean Sea.

Moses smote the rock and out gushed forth water. Jesus was the rock that was smitten and out gushed torrents of living water.

Moses fed the people manna from heaven. Jesus, the true manna from heaven, fed the multitudes.

Moses ushered in the first covenant. Jesus authored the final covenant!

This incomplete list of many of the similitudes between Moses and Jesus unfortunately has been missed by the Jews. In our day today, they continue to elevate Moses while persisting to dismiss Jesus as a mere false Messiah. The book of Zechariah tells us though that this will not always be the case.

> And I will pour upon the house of David, and upon the inhabitants of Jerusalem, the spirit of grace and supplications: And they shall look upon me whom they have pierced, and they shall mourn for him, as one mourneth for his only son, and shall be in bitterness for him, as one that is in bitterness for his firstborn.
>
> Zechariah 12:10

In that day, the Jews will finally fulfill Moses's words. They will see Jesus as the prophet like Moses, and they will hearken unto him.

As an application to this section, I would like to take a look at the damnable sin of envy, for both Moses and Jesus were envied by the people with personal and corporate disaster as its result.

> And Miriam and Aaron spake against Moses...and they said, hath the Lord indeed spoken only by Moses? Hath he not spoken also by us? And the Lord heard it.
>
> Numbers 12:1–2

Envy is wanting something that somebody else has. It is the opposite of contentment! Often, it is camouflaged by words that misdirect a listener from a person's true motives. Words of criticism, humor, or "valid concerns" are often a smokescreen hiding a person's real feelings of envy.

God hates envy! In Miriam's case, she became leprous and was shut up, separated from the camp of Israel for seven days. During that time, the people were put on hold unable to travel forward.

God is serious about envy. This example tells me that envy is sin (leprosy always pictures sin in the Bible). Envy separates and isolates people, and it holds others back in the process.

> Now Korah...and Dathan and Abiram...took men. And they rose up before Moses, with certain of the children of Israel, two hundred and fifty princes of the assembly, famous in the congregation, men of renown:
>
> Numbers 16:1–2

Envy has a way of sucking others into its web! As you will see, the end is not good for those who are so trapped!

> And they gathered themselves against Moses and against Aaron, and said unto them, Ye take too much upon you, seeing all the congregation is holy, every one of them, and the Lord is among them: Wherefore then lift ye up yourselves above the congregation of the Lord?
>
> Numbers 16:3

Masked as a valid concern, the multitude railed against God's men in saying they were self-promoting themselves over the people. Their fallacious argument was that God gifts all men equally! It doesn't take much of a student of the Bible to know that that isn't true!

> And when Moses heard it...he spake unto Korah, and unto all his company, saying, Even tomorrow the Lord will show who are his, and who is holy...And the Lord spake unto Moses saying, Speak unto the congregation, saying, Get you up from about the tabernacle of Korah, Dathan and Abiram...And he spake unto the congregation, saying, depart, I pray you, from the tents of these wicked men, and touch nothing of theirs, lest ye be consumed in all their sins.
>
> Numbers 16:4–5, 23–26

Envy will consume a man or a woman. God is clearly telling you and me to depart from the envious person, lest we be wiped out also!

> So they got up from the tabernacle of Korah, Dathan and Abiram, on every side: And Dathan and Abiram came out, and stood in the door of their tents, and their wives, and their sons, and their little children.
>
> Numbers 16:27

We are about to see how sin has repercussions we don't consider. In this case, the three confederates will also be taking out their entire families! Even the little kids! Mom and Dad, your sins don't just affect you. They stink up your kids too. I want to remember this as God tells me that the wages of sin is death (Romans 6:23). Death to self, death to relationships, and death to families!

> And Moses said, Hereby ye shall know that the Lord hath sent me to do all these works; for I have not done them of mine own mind. If these men die the common death of all men...then the Lord hath not sent me. But if the Lord make a new thing, and the earth open her mouth, and swallow them up, with all that belong to them, and they go down quick into the pit; then ye shall understand that these men have provoked the Lord. And it came to pass as he made an end of speaking all these words, that the ground clave asunder that was under them: And the earth opened her mouth and swallowed them up, and their houses, and all the men that belonged into Korah, and all their goods. They and all that belonged to them, went down alive into the pit, and the earth closed upon them: And they perished from among the congregation... And there came out a fire from the Lord, and consumed the two hundred and fifty men.
>
> Numbers 16:28–33, 35

Not good! Paul tells you and me that the Old Testament stories are meant as examples for us living in the New Testament age of grace (1 Corinthians 10:11). We are to see that God is deadly serious about envy. It's the pits! Envy will lead to disaster. It will spread, and it will kill. And there will always be collateral damage!

Like Moses, in Jesus' day, the Jews made the same error.

> For he (Pontius Pilate) knew that for envy they had delivered him (Jesus).
>
> Matthew 27:18

> For he knew that the chief priests had delivered him for envy.
>
> Mark 15:10

The Jewish leaders also wanted what was rightfully our Lord's. They wanted to lead the nation; they wanted the best seats at the feasts; and they wanted the glory and honor. They envied the Messiah as God gave to him what they so desperately wanted!

And like Miriam, Korah, Dathan, and Abiram, they too were eaten up and taken out!

> And when he had come near, he beheld the city [Jerusalem], and wept over it. Saying, if thou hadst known, even thou, at least in this thy day, the things which belong unto thy peace! But now they are hid from your eyes [your envy has blinded you from seeing]. For the days shall come upon thee, that thine enemies shall cast a trench about thee, and compass thee round, and keep thee in on every side, and shall lay thee even with the ground, and thy children within thee; and they shall not leave in thee one stone upon another; because thou knewest not the time of thy visitation.
>
> Luke 19:41–44

Thirty-five years later, this prophecy came to pass. Jerusalem was burnt, the temple was leveled, and the children were killed. Jesus revealed that it was entirely due to the fact that the leaders of the nation missed it! And they missed it because they envied the Savior when they should have worshipped him!

So the take home point is that I must never envy, I must never lust in my heart after a gift that someone over me has been given by God. I need to watch out for the camouflage of criticism, humor, and "valid concerns," and most importantly, I want to give thanks for the gifts the giver has given to me as well as to those that I might be tempted to envy.

For further study:

1. Can you remember any times you used the smokescreen of "valid concerns" to hide your true feelings toward another?

2. Is there anyone in your life whose envy towards another is affecting you? What should you do about that?

3. Has sin in your life ever caused "collateral damage" you weren't anticipating?

AARON: THE HIGH PRIEST

Moses's brother Aaron was the first high priest to the nation. In this capacity, he pictures the great high priest, Jesus Christ. The role of the high priest was two-fold. First, he was to represent God before the people, i.e. be a witness. Second, he was to stand before God for the people, that is, intercession. Of course, we see that in Jesus. "He who has seen me has seen the Father" Jesus proclaimed. He is the perfect witness of the Father! And, Jesus ever lives to make intercession for the saints (Hebrews 7:25). Like the high priest, Jesus stands before the Father on our behalf.

In the Bible, the anointing oil pictures the Holy Spirit. We are told of Aaron that Moses "poured of the anointing oil upon Aaron's head, and anointed him, to sanctify him" (Leviticus 8:12). Likewise, the spiritual anointing given to Christ and his body of believing saints was seen in a description of Aaron found in one of David's songs.

Behold how good and how pleasant it is for brethren to dwell together in unity! It is like the precious ointment upon the head, that ran down upon the beard, even Aaron's beard: That went down to the skirts of his garments.

Psalm 133:1–2

Aaron's head and beard typify Christ in this psalm. Christ is the head. Of course, the oil continued down to the skirts of Aaron's garments, that is, the spirit also flows down to the body, the entity that we are told in Ephesians is the church.

Lastly, before we leave Aaron and his ties to the great high priest, we must mention the rod that budded forth fruit.

In the book of Numbers, we find the account of the wilderness wanderings of the children of Israel. Rebellion, disobedience, envy, and murmuring seemed to be the staple for God's kids during that time. Thus, an entire generation was not able to enter into the promised land. In studying this book, one can learn about the pitfalls of carnality in our Christian walk that can bring us down and wipe us out! As I, in my lack of faith and commitment stray away from God's plan for my life by my rebellion, disobedience, envying, and complaining, I too will miss out on the promises of God for my life just like that generation of Israel missed out on entering into the land of promise.

One of those lessons and the picture I want you to see is found in chapter 17 where we learn of Aaron's rod, which budded. The people were envious of Moses's and Aaron's authority, feeling that they certainly must be glory hogs, lusting for power and authority over the people. This thought, of course, was not from the Father. So God told Moses to take rods, one for Aaron and one each for the heads of the twelve tribes. Then he said to place those rods in the tabernacle overnight, and the rod of the one that God has chosen would blossom and bear fruit. We know that it was Aaron's rod that miraculously brought forth fruit! In this we see our Lord. He too was and is envied. Those in the world question why Jesus is the only way. Like the budding of only Aaron's rod, we know that Jesus was and is the only one who like that dead stick, came back to life! Jesus, the rod of the stem of Jesse, was disconnected from his Father, the source of all life, yet he came back to life just as did Aaron's rod. All other roads to God can and are seen as those other dead rods, which had no fruit. Only Jesus is the fruit-bearing rod. Jesus is Aaron's rod, and certainly, he must have told that to those men on the road to Emmaus.

For further study:

1. We in the New Testament are called a royal priesthood. Thus, we are witnesses for God. How has he called you to be his witness?

2. Jesus is seen as the fruit-bearing rod. Can you think of any examples of "dead sticks" which claim to have authority from God?

3. Is the philosophy that all religions lead to God biblical? Does this story bolster that point of view or crush it?

JOSHUA: THE CAPTAIN
OF ISRAEL'S HOST

JOSHUA, MOSES'S MINISTER, was a wonderful
Old Testament picture of our Lord Jesus Christ. Joshua led the
children of Israel into the promised land just as the greater than
Joshua leads God's kids into the promised land of the spirit-filled
life. Joshua definitely was spoken of on that holy road that day!

I have written about General Joshua's ties to Jesus in my pre-
vious two books. Let me show you an excerpt from book two of a
Woman's Silent Testimony,

> Now, Joshua, wonderful Joshua! We must speak of him.
>
> His name means "Jehovah saves." Throughout the
> Bible, he is a wonderful and powerful picture of the greater
> than Joshua, Jesus Christ. In fact, we know Jesus by his
> Greek name of Jesus, but this is not a name people actually
> called him during his earthly life. His name in Aramaic is

Yeshua. That's how people knew him. The Hebrew translation is Joshua!

Yes, Joshua led the people into the Promised Land, just as Jesus leads us into the promised land of the Spirit-filled life, into the land of the new covenant walk. Into the land, as Jeremiah 31:33 points out, where God writes his will upon our hearts.

Understanding Joshua's role in this story gives us a beautiful picture of God's plan of salvation. You see, Moses represents the Law, the Ten Commandments, the Old Testament. Joshua represents Jesus, the New Covenant, the Age of Grace. The Law, as we have discussed earlier, is our schoolmaster to bring us to Christ. It is the ten camels that Rebekah rode to find Isaac that we ride to find our greater than Isaac, Jesus Christ. It brings us to the Promised Land, but Jesus brings us in. When we get to the Promised Land, we are no longer under the Law but under grace. We go from the Old Covenant of rules and regulations to the New Covenant of grace, the place where we have God's will written upon our hearts! Yes, God wonderfully paints a picture in passing the leadership of his people from Moses to Joshua.

A Woman's Silent Testimony: 77-78

In addition to Joshua being a strong prototype of Jesus in relation to our savior's first coming to planet earth, Joshua's story also speaks of Christ's second coming and, specifically, of Jesus' physically taking back the world as seen in the book of Revelation. That is, Joshua's campaign to take the promised land back from the kings of Canaan is revisited again by Jesus' crusade to take the world back from Satan and the end-times world-wide king known as the Antichrist.

Early in the book of Joshua, we see the General sending in two spies who spoke to Rahab and were hidden for three days (a picture of death) before returning back to Joshua. In the Revelation, Jesus will send the two witnesses to call believers out of Jerusalem. They will subsequently be killed and will lay dead for three days before coming back to life, ascending up in front of all, and returning back to him.

Concomitant with sending out the two spies, Joshua, as the captain of Israel's host, had an encounter with an awesome figure, which the Bible calls the "Captain of the Lord's Host." Zechariah 14:1–4 reveals that Jesus is that captain of the Lord's host, who Joshua encountered on that day!

Again early in his book, Joshua had his warriors encircle Jericho where they blew the trumpet and shouted. Immediately the walls fell down and the Bible states that the men of Israel "ascended up" and took the city. Likewise, at the beginning of the tribulation time frame, we men of Israel (Israel means "governed by God") will also hear a shout and a trump (1 Thessalonians 4:16–17) and we too will ascend up in the event we understand to be the rapture of the church.

Joshua made a pact with a group of Gentiles known as the Gibeonites who were theretofore destined to be taken out. The Gibeonites came to Joshua in humility and broke bread and shared wine with him causing Joshua to spare their lives and to actually protect them from their enemies. True to the type, Jesus will spare the Gentile converts who come to him in humility, communing with him by taking his body and blood during the end-times campaign, which he will lead.

The drive to take back the promised land took seven years (Joshua 14:7–10). The tribulation time frame is also recognized to be seven years.

Joshua took on the leader of the Canaanites known as Adonizedek. *Adoni* means "lord," and *zedek* is translated *right-eousness*. Adonizedek was the king of Jerusalem. Now this is interesting. Here we have Joshua who we understand to be a type of Jesus taking on Adonizedek whose name means "lord of right-eousness" and who is the king of Jerusalem. I hope you can see that Adonizedek is a near-perfect picture of that future world king known as the Antichrist. Indeed, the Antichrist will proclaim himself to be the lord of righteousness and will seek to be the king of Jerusalem. Likewise, he too will take on the greater than Joshua in those latter-day battles.

During the battle to take back the promised land, the Bible tells us that the kings hid themselves in the cave at Makkedah to flee from the wrath of Joshua (Joshua 11:16). Likewise, we learn in Revelation that the kings of the earth will hide themselves in dens and in the rocks to retreat from the face of him that sitteth on the throne and from the wrath of the Lamb (Revelation 6:15–16).

Joshua spoke to the sun and the moon, and their motion stopped (Joshua 10:12). Again, during the seven-year time of Jacob's trouble (Jeremiah 30:7) we will see signs in the sun and the moon as Jesus prophesied in Matthew 24:29.

Lastly, at the end of Joshua's campaign to take the promised land we read,

> And the Lord gave them rest round about, according to all that he sware unto their fathers: And there stood not a man of all their enemies before them; the Lord delivered all their enemies into their hand. There failed not ought of any good thing which the Lord had spoken unto the house of Israel; *all came to pass.* (emphasis mine)
>
> Joshua 21:44–45

After the future enemy is defeated we will hear,

> Behold, the tabernacle of God is with men, and he will dwell with them, and they shall be his people, and God himself shall be with them, and be their God. And God shall wipe away all tears from their eyes; and there shall be no more death, neither sorrow, nor crying, neither shall there be any more pain: *For the former things are passed away.* (emphasis mine)
>
> Revelation 21:3–4

What a day that will be!

Now before we leave the story of how Joshua typifies Jesus Christ, an application is pulling at me. Before General Joshua became the captain of the Israel's host, he was the minister of Moses. He was his servant (Joshua 1:1). Likewise, before Jesus ascended on high as King of kings and Lord of lords, he too came to serve. I think of that night in the room of the last supper when our Lord girded himself and washed the disciples' feet. Think about that, the creator of the universe (Hebrews 1:2) took the form of a slave and washed the feet of those who were under him! In that context of service, he taught that if one is to be great in the Kingdom of God he will be as a servant (John 13:12-17). And that's the point, that's the thing I must remember. If I want to be great, if I want to ascend on high, I must *desire* to serve others.

It's not about people serving and waiting on me, it's about me giving of myself to others. Well, how do I get to that place, that holy zone, where I sacrificially desire to serve others you may say? The answer to that profound and important question is the key to receiving God's grace. It's by remembering and being amazed by what the savior did for you, what he did for me. He went to the cross and saved us from hell! So as we remember that and serve as the response to that, then we will be great in the kingdom of God!

For further study:

1. Jesus was called Yeshua while he walked the earth, yet he has many names & titles. What are your favorites?

2. The walls of Jericho seemed impregnable to the children of Israel, yet God dramatically toppled them after the army marched around the city for seven days. Has God ever moved in a moment of the miraculous, knocking down walls in your life that loomed large & imposing?

3. Do you find it a blessing or a burden to serve others? What types of activities can you do for others which you enjoy? Okay, that's what you should be doing! Psalm 37:4

THE JUDGES:
GLIMPSES OF JESUS

THE JUDGES OF Israel certainly were spoken of by Jesus to those two men on the road to Emmaus. The Hebrew word for *judge* can also be translated *deliverer*. Indeed, *deliverer* is a more accurate rendering as reading their stories revealed. Their number was twelve from the book with the same name and fourteen if we include Eli and Samuel (which we should). Of course, twelve and fourteen are holy numbers used exactingly by God to present spiritual truths—twelve being the number of Israel (those who are governed by God) and fourteen representing the establishment of spiritual perfection (combining two and seven).

Each judge of Israel pictured a partial truth revealing the character and ministry of the one being revealed. Taken together, they painted a beautiful portrait of our deliverer, Jesus Christ. Let's take a look at these men (and one woman) and see how they point to the savior.

OTHNIEL: LOOKING FOR GOD

The first Judge was Othniel, the nephew of Caleb. His name means "looking for God," and in his account found in Judges 3, we learn that he was filled with the Spirit and went to war against Israel's enemies. Likewise, at the beginning of Jesus' earthly ministry, the people were also looking for God. John declared, "Behold the Lamb of God who taketh away the sin of the world"(John 1:29). On that day, Jesus too was filled with the Spirit as he came out of the waters of baptism. That filling equipped him to go out into the wilderness, where he battled against the enemy not only of Israel but of all men. The enemy we know to be Satan!

EHUD: THE LEFT-HANDED MAN

The second Judge was a man named Ehud. Ehud was from the tribe of Benjamin, and we were told that he was left-handed. This additional information can be missed but is germane to the story. Remember, the name Benjamin means "son of my right arm," the right hand being the hand of blessing. So in Ehud's name, we see the humility of Jesus in his humanity. Indeed, the second person of the triune Godhead is the Son of the Father's right arm, but he came to the world sort of left-handed, didn't he? Born in a manger, raised in Galilee, he was not what the people expected in the deliverer!

Ehud assassinated the king of Moab by taking a sword and thrusting it into the belly of that king. The Bible states that the "dirt came out!"(Judges 3:22). This is a nice way of saying that all of the gross contents that we flush down the toilet when we elim-inate our fleshly waste came rushing out of the mortal wound! It was bad; it was smelly. It was actually sort of comical though as the Bible tells us that the king's servants delayed their discovery of the dead monarch because they only thought he was using the bathroom (Judges 3:24)!

Of course, the Bible teaches in multiple places that the Word of God is likened to a sword (Ephesians 6:17, Hebrews 4:12). Whenever we see a sword, dagger, or knife being spoken of in the Old Testament, there will be a New Testament principle or application embedded therein. In this case, we can see how the word of God goes in and out comes the dirt of our sin! The word goes in and out comes my sin. As I feed on the words of the author of all creation, I get rid of that sin and stink; otherwise, it continues to build up in my life. Truly and reverently, the Word is like a laxative. We take it in, and we get cleaned out and freshened up!

Lastly, in Othniel we saw how Jesus is filled with the Spirit for battle. In Ehud, we see a picture of how the power of the word of God was displayed in Jesus for combat. When Jesus met the enemy of Israel, when he met who the king of Moab typifies, he too used the word of God as his dagger to take down the strong man. In each of the recorded temptations, the one Ehud pictures took the sword in his clash against Satan. Truly, the word of God is an offensive weapon (Ephesians 6:17)!

SHAMGAR: OBEDIENT SON

The third judge was a man by the name of Shamgar. Let's look at his story as it is only one verse. But what a one-liner it is!

> And after him [Ehud] was Shamgar the son of Anath, which slew of the Philistines six hundred men with an ox goad: He also delivered Israel.
>
> Judges 3:31

Shamgar, whose name means "obedient son," whose father was Anath (the name of the sister of Baal who was the Canaanite goddess of love), used what was in his hand, an ox goad, to overcome the Philistines. Likewise, Jesus, "the obedient son," came to this earth under the shadow of the fornication of his mother and used what was in his hand (the cross) to slay the Philistine (Satan)!

Shamgar completed a three-fold picture, for in his victory, we see how service will bring the triumph. He used what was in his hand. He used what he knew. He used his abilities as a farmer to take out the enemy. That's what serving others will do for me also. As I give out, I actually receive back! Jesus said it best in John 13:17 when he said in the context of service, "If ye know these things, *happy* are ye if ye *do* them" (emphasis mine). If I want to be happy, then I need to do what the teacher says. In Shamgar, he is saying to serve others.

So we see in the first three judges the power of the Spirit, the power of the word, and the power of service to others in taking down the kingdom of the god of this world (2 Corinthians 4:4). This also was what Jesus displayed in his life and ministry for all to see!

DEBORAH: A MOTHER IN ISRAEL

The fourth judge was Deborah. She was a prophet and called herself a mother in Israel (Judges 5:7). As the only female judge, she portrays a side of the redeemer that we sometimes overlook— his feminine side, his tender side. Deborah was used to inspire a timid general named Barak into action. She told Barak that God would fight the battle for them over the superior Canaanite forces of their day. Barak was reluctant but did eventually believe and went to battle. True to her prophetic word, the Lord sent a powerful rainstorm (during the dry season) that entrapped the Canaanite army and allowed Barak and the men of Israel of obtain the victory. Likewise, Jesus, as God, is called "El Shaddai." Shad is derived from the Hebrew word for breast. Jesus as El (masculine) is also Shaddai (feminine)! He is both. He is complete. For the judges to portray partial revelations of Jesus, then of course, a woman would need to be included in the picture. For Jesus is in touch with his feminine side! Like a mother to her children, he says to you and me,

Come to me, all ye that labor and are heavy laden, and I will give you rest. Take my yoke upon you and learn of me; for I am meek and lowly in heart: And ye shall find rest unto your souls. For my yoke is easy, and my burden is light.

Matthew 11:28–30

GIDEON: THE LIGHT HIDDEN IN AN EARTHEN VESSEL

Gideon is a name with which we are all familiar. "He who cuts" is what Gideon means. Indeed, in reading the story of the fifth judge, we can see that Gideon, once he believed that God would use him to deliver the people from the Midianites, became a man on a mission. He was no-nonsense. Gideon seemed to always cut right to the chase. He would get right to the point! In one night, he pulled down the altar to Baal that his father and the men of the town had erected (Judges 6:25–27). In routing the Midianites, he was not satisfied in the sending them away after 120,000 men of their ranks were destroyed. No he and his three hundred men chased after the survivors. Comically, that was fifteen thousand men that were running away from him! The two cities that refused to help during the pursuit received the chastisement, which Gideon promised to them on his victorious return from the battle (Judges 8:4–17).

Likewise, our Lord is no-nonsense. He is a consuming fire. He is not a respecter of persons! I think of the time when the master, in righteous anger, overthrew the tables of the money changers as they were fleecing the worshipers and, thereby, polluting his Father's house. Jesus' word will cut to the point. His word is true. Like Gideon, Jesus is able to discern the thoughts and intents of the heart (Hebrews 4:12)!

But there is another powerful picture for us to see, which Jesus certainly mentioned to those two blessed men on the road to

Emmaus concerning Gideon. That is, in the battle to free Israel from the Midianites, Jesus in his humanity is clearly seen. Gideon told his three hundred men to put their lamps in earthen vessels for their nighttime attack. This would keep them from being seen as they snuck up upon their enemies. He also gave them trumpets to blow. At the right moment, they all broke their earthen vessels, letting the light shine forth brightly. Simultaneously, from all sides of the Midianite camp, they blew their trumpets. The usurpers of Israel undoubtedly thought they were being overrun by a larger force and, in their stupor, began killing each other.

This is the savior's story also. God became a man. He became an earthen vessel if you will. He was the light of the world, yet it was sort of hidden in the body of a man whom the Bible says had no form or comeliness that we should desire him (Isaiah 53:2).

Then that earthen vessel was broken, letting the light shine forth on the cross of Calvary. Jesus trumpeted the victory three days later in rising from the dead. Inconceivably, the victory was obtained against incredible odds just as in Gideon's day!

TOLA: THE SCARLET WORM

The sixth Judge is one of my favorites. We are told that Tola was a defender of God's people (Judges 10:1–2). As is often the case in the Bible, the name once again gives the connection. It tells the story for Tola means "worm." Tola is a specific type of worm found in the Middle East that is absurdly cool when you learn about its significance. A tola worm is colored red, and after living its wormy life, it reproduces in death! Now it's time to start thinking how we are going to tie this to Jesus, dear reader, as the story gets even better. In death, this red worm climbs a tree and dies as the baby worms are delivered. In its demise, the tola covers the baby worms, and then after three days, falls off the tree, leaving a white mark!

So do you see the picture? A blood-red worm climbed a tree to give birth, died on that tree as she covered her children, and left a white mark on the tree three days later. This was Jesus' sacrifice perfectly! The savior shed his scarlet blood as he too climbed on that tree in birthing us into his kingdom. His blood covered and completely washed away our sin, turning us white like that mark he left three days later when he rose from the dead, confirming that his sacrifice was accepted by God. Truly, Jesus is Tola, our defender!

But there is one more powerful prophetic connection to say about Tola that could not have been missed on that road to Emmaus. In Psalm 22, the crucifixion psalm, David, in his travail, spoke not only of himself, but also of the one he so wonderfully portrayed as we will later see. He said,

> But I am a worm [Tola] and no man; a reproach of men, and despised of the people. All they that see me laugh me to scorn: They shoot out the lip, they shake the head, saying, He trusted on the Lord that he would deliver him: Let him deliver him, seeing he delighted in him.
>
> Psalm 22:6–8

Jesus, our savior and friend, became the Tola, he became the worm. Think about that. God becoming a man is like you and me changing ourselves into worms! This sort of demotion is unthinkable! Yet that's exactly what he did. He became a red worm and climbed the tree so we could live forever with him. Praise Yahweh for that indescribable sacrifice!

JAIR: GOD IS LIGHT

"He gives light" is the meaning of Jair's name. Of course, in the name alone, we see the tie to the Messiah, the light of the world (John 1:1–9). But Jair also had thirty sons who were deputized by their father to judge over the people (Judges 10:3–5). In this, we see an important ministry that we, as God's children, are and will be given. We too have been commissioned by God to take the gospel to the people today (2 Corinthians 5:18–20). And we too will rule and reign with Jesus in the ages to come (Revelation 5:10, 22:3–4). Again, in this seventh judge, we see a partial glimpse of the ministry of Jesus Christ!

JEPHTHAH: BORN OF FORNICATION

The eighth deliverer of Israel was Jephthah, a man whose name means "Yahweh frees." The Bible states that Jephthah was a mighty man of valor. He was a warrior! But Jephthah was also the son of a harlot. Jephthah's father's wife begat him many sons, and those sons in their superiority and self-righteous promotion said unto Jephthah, "Thou shalt not inherit in our father's house; for thou are the son of a strange woman" (Judges 11:2). They thrust him out, and Jephthah fled from his brethren and dwelt in the land of Tob.

This is also what we saw in Jesus. His brothers, the Jewish leaders, said of Jesus that he was born of fornication while they were not (John 8:41). They too did not want to share the Father's inheritance with Jesus, their brother. They thrust him out of the nation, and the one whom Jephthah typifies also went to the land of Tob (the meaning of Tob is "good"). That is, Jesus ascended to heaven, that good place, where he sits at the right hand of the Father.

> And it came to pass in the process of time, that the children of Ammon made war against Israel. And it was so, that when the children of Ammon made war against Israel, the elders of Gilead [Jephthah's brothers] went to fetch Jephthah out of the land of Tob [modern-day Syria]: And they said unto Jephthah, Come, and be our captain, that we may fight with the children of Ammon.
>
> Judges 11:4–6

In this, we see a prophetic picture of what those future brothers of Jesus will do in the latter days when the people the children of Ammon portray, the Antichrist and his leagues, will once again make war against Israel. In that day, Jesus' brothers will call upon him to return and lead them against the Ammonite just as they did in the days of Jephthah!

IBZAN: HOUSE OF BREAD

The birthplace of Ibzan is the prophetic picture that this deliverer portrays.

> And after him Ibzan of Bethlehem judged Israel.
>
> Judges 12:8

Bethlehem, also the prophesied birthplace of the Messiah (Micah 5:2), means "house of bread." Indeed, with a name such as that, from what better place would the bread of life (John 6:35) enter into the world?

ELON: HE WILL RECEIVE HONOR

The Bible teaches that Elon was a man from Zebulon. In hailing from the land of Zebulon, we see a glimpse of the savior. The meaning of the name of this sixth son of Leah was "honor" as Leah hoped she would finally be honored over her rival, Rachel, in that she had given Jacob six sons. Yet this was not really the case. Leah was not the favorite of Jacob, and thus, Zebulon was a "lesser son," if you will. Later, in the dividing of the promised land after Joshua's victories, the land that the tribe of Zebulon inherited was in the north, far from the spiritual center of the nation down in the south. In Jesus' day, the Jews believed he was from Zebulon. We know, like Ibzan, that our Lord was born in Bethlehem, but the Jews supposed he was a lesser son stemming from the non-important land of Zebulon. The Jews "knew" they had all of the facts. The messiah would be the son of David, yet this "false messiah" was a son of Zebulon, born in Nazareth, or so they thought! In their blindness, they forgot the words of Isaiah,

> The land of Zebulon and the land of Naphtali...beyond Jordan, in Galilee of the nations. The people that walked in darkness have seen a great light: They that dwell in the land of the shadow of death, upon them hath the light shined.
>
> Isaiah 9:1–2

Zebulon, the son Leah who hoped would bring honor to her, was ultimately lifted up and honored in nurturing and bringing forth Jesus, the man from Galilee, the great light that shined forth unto the Jews, and unto us also, who dwell in this land of the shadow of death!

ABDON: SERVANT

The meaning of the name of the eleventh judge is "servant." Not too hard to see a picture of the Son of Man in the name of Abdon. As the Bible proclaims, "For even the Son of man came not to be ministered unto (*served*), but to minister (*serve*), and to give his life a ransom for many" (Mark 10:45).

SAMSON: THE HE MAN WITH A SHE WEAKNESS

At first thought, one would wonder how Samson would be an appropriate type or picture of the Lord. After all, in reading Samson's story, we see an arrogant man who really had a problem with the ladies! Sure, he was blessed by God with strength, and the name Samson means "strong," but come on, he had some real issues! Well, remember, theses judges show glimpses of Jesus. No one deliverer has the entire package. In Samson's case, we see Jesus in his death.

After Samson was called on the carpet, so to speak, by God for his continued disregard of his Nazarite vows in his dealings with the temptress, Delilah, he was blinded and taken by the Philistines. There he was put to work, grinding wheat at the miller's wheel. Over the process of time, his hair began to grow back, and unbeknownst to him, God's blessing was about to be bestowed. Samson knew he had failed as the judge of Israel. He was a captive. He was a spectacle to the enemies of Israel. He was a laughingstock, and he caused the Philistines to give praise to their God, who they believed had brought them the victory. But on the day they were celebrating and making merry, the Philistines brought Samson into the temple of their God to make "sport" of him. It was then, in his humility and death that Samson portrayed our hero.

Samson asked the lad who held him to lead him to the two pillars of the house. There he prayed to God for one last powerful move of the spirit in his life. God granted the request, and Samson stretched out his arms and toppled the pillars of the temple. The house fell in upon itself, and Samson slew the enemies of Israel in his death. That's of course what Jesus did too, isn't it? Jesus, in humility and apparent weakness, was taken in to the temple of the enemy (Calvary) and stretched forth his arms in dying. In doing so, he too took down his enemy (Satan) with a show of strength that could never be equaled!

ELI: YAHWEH IS EXALTED

From the first book of Samuel, we find the last two judges of Israel. They too typify our friend. The commonality we see in Eli is in his name, "Yahweh is exalted," and in his position, Eli was the high priest of Israel.

SAMUEL: GIVEN TO GOD

In the last judge of Israel and first of the prophetic writers after Moses, we see several associations with the true last judge of Israel. Scholars are divided on the interpretation of his name. Yet the three schools of thought are all beautiful. "Heard of God" is one interpretation. In hearing God, Jesus stated that he always did the will of the Father. Another rendering of the name Samuel is "his name is God." Of course Jesus said "I and my Father are one" (John 10:30). The last version of the prophet's name is "the unnamed God is El." In this, I think of the time that Moses asked God to tell him his name (Exodus 3:13). Also from the book of Revelation, we will see the King of kings and Lord of lords come back to the earth, "And he had a name written, that no man knew, but he himself" (Revelation 19:12). Truly Jesus is the unnamed God!

The birth of Samuel also ties him to the Messiah. Samuel's mother, Hannah, was barren. She wanted a son to give to her husband. In her desperation, she prayed to have a son, and in return, she promised the unnamed God that she would give the child back to him all the days of his life. That's the prayer that had power. For God wanted a son, not to give to her husband but a son to give to the nation! In Jesus, we can see the same thing. Like Hannah, Israel had become barren. Spiritual fruit was not being produced in the nation. Then along came Emanuel! Jesus, "God with us," was not only given to the nation, but he was given by God to all of humanity!

So we see how the fourteen judges of Israel, some famous and some obscure, all give us glimpses of our Lord and would have been mentioned by him as he listed the many, many ties to him from the Old Testament to those two men on the road to Emmaus. But there is an application for us that these deliverers suggest. God needed to raise up these men in each case because the people had fallen back, had walked away, had succumbed to idolatry and sin. In their series of stories, a recurring theme of sin followed by supplication to God was in play. I don't want that for my life! It shouldn't have to be for yours! I want to live life without having to always be rescued by God because of my many miscues! The book of Jude tells me how I can succeed in this desire.

> But ye, beloved, building up yourselves on your most holy faith, praying in the Holy Ghost, keep yourselves in the love of God, looking for the mercy of our Lord Jesus Christ unto eternal life.
>
> Jude 20–21

I want to keep myself in the love of God by remembering and doing three things. First, build myself up in my most holy faith—that's staying in God's word. Second, praying in the Holy Ghost—that's praying in the Spirit. Third, looking for the mercy of our Lord Jesus Christ unto eternal life—that's looking and longing for his return! Three things—the word, prayer, and the hope of Christ's return can keep you and me from straying away like a lost sheep that Jesus always needs to leave and rescue back to the flock.

For further study:

1. Being left-handed was considered a curse in bible days yet it was turned to a blessing as the men of Moab did not look for a weapon that a left-handed man would use before giving Ehud an audience with Eglon. Have you ever had a seeming curse in your life actually turned into a blessing? How did God orchestrate that curse into a blessing?

2. Jesus is both masculine & feminine. He is awesome yet he is meek & lowly. He is a consuming fire yet the little children readily approached him. How does the paradoxical Jesus make you feel about him? Is he scary to you or gentle & friendly? Is he both?

3. Jesus was misunderstood by the Jews who believed he was
    from Zebulon when in fact he was born in Bethlehem.
    But in reading the gospel accounts it is clear that he never
    really argued against their misconception of him. Is there
    a lesson for you & me in that story when we are misunder-
    stood by those who would want to harm our reputation?

BOAZ: THE KINSMAN REDEEMER

THE LITTLE BOOK of Ruth contains a powerful allegory concerning Israel, the church, and our savior, Jesus Christ.
During the days of the judges of Israel, a time when the Bible
states, "There was no king in Israel; every man did that which
was right in his own eyes" (Judges 21:25), there was a famine in
the land.

Thus, a man named Elimelech took his wife, whose name was
Naomi, and their two sons and left their home in Bethlehem
Judah and traveled east to Moab, looking for relief. There, the two
boys married Moabite women, one of whom was named Ruth.
Soon thereafter, Elimelech and his sons died, leaving Naomi
and the two daughter-in-laws alone. Naomi, in her broken state,
decided to return back to Bethlehem when she learned that God
had visited his people with bread. One of the daughters, Ruth,

desired to travel with her. When Naomi returned, she told the people of Bethlehem to now call her Mara. In their poverty back in Judah, Naomi instructed Ruth to glean in the fields during the barley harvest as was the custom in those days. While gleaning, Ruth was seen by Boaz who was the owner of the field where Ruth was working. It turned out that Boaz was a respected and wise landowner, the holder of a vast fortune. Boaz approached Ruth and blessed her with gifts. In response, Ruth requested Boaz to cover and protect her as he was a near kinsman. This was what Boaz desired to do the moment he saw her weeks earlier, but in order to redeem Ruth, he needed a closer kinsman of hers to give up his rights to her. Indeed, that nearer relative was unable to redeem Ruth, and thus, he gave over the right of redemption to Boaz. The two were married, and they brought Ruth's mother-in-law Naomi into the covering of the family as well.

What a story! The Jews celebrate it to this day, yet prophetically, they do not understand it at all. On the road to Emmaus, Jesus must have opened the two men's eyes to this wonderful story as he explained to them that Boaz spoke of himself.

Let's break it down. Naomi's name means "pleasant." She and her family left Bethlehem Judah during a time of famine and traveled to Moab. Ironically, Bethlehem means "house of bread" and Judah means "praise." The Bible calls Moab, God's wash pot, i.e. toilet! So we see in the names that Mrs. Pleasant left the place of praise and bread in a time of dryness to go live in the outhouse! This is what happened to Israel. They too were pleasant and blessed as they praised God and feasted upon the bread of his word. But then they left the Lord in days of hardship, and the people died off just as did Elimelech and his two sons. When Naomi returned, she said to call her Mara, meaning "bitter." This typifies what has happened to the nation historically. They too have become embittered. But, when Naomi's Gentile daughter-in-law Ruth was seen by Boaz, all began to be made right! Boaz means "in him is strength," and he powerfully pictures the redeemer, Jesus Christ. Ruth, who as a picture of the believing church of Christ, asked Boaz for his covering (a picture of accepting Jesus as Lord). He, of course, agreed. First though, Boaz needed to obtain the rights to her as there was one who had greater claim to her than did he. That relative typifies the law. We are all under the law, and the Bible states we are damned by it as we have woefully fallen so short of its requirements. Jesus died for us and obtained the rights to our souls, his Gentile bride, just as Boaz needed to sacrifice in order to procure the rights to Ruth from the nearer relative who was unwilling and unable to redeem Ruth as his wife. In the end of the story, Naomi is brought into the family just as Israel will be at the end of this age! Truly Jesus is Boaz. In him is strength. He is our redeemer, and like Boaz, he has rescued us in the time of our poverty and from our ownership to the law. And he will bring Israel back to him in the days to come!

As an application, look spiritually at what Elimelech and Naomi did. In their time of famine, they left Bethlehem. They left the promised land. I don't want to let that happen to me. I don't want it for you! When times of spiritual dryness come, I must stay put. I need to keep in the place of praise and in the house of bread. That is, I need to be with God's people. I need to be in church where praise is ascending and the bread of his word is given out. And I must stay in the land of his promises. God states that as I travel with him, he will never leave me nor forsake me. But what happens if I walk away? We see that the book of Ruth gives the answer. Things in my life will die, and once again, he will need to supernaturally rescue me!

For further study:

1. Where is the best place for you to be in times of famine, in times of spiritual dryness in your life?

2. The names of the men in Naomi's life add color to the story. "God is king" is the meaning of Elimelech. Mahlon means "song" & Chilion means "satisfaction." Look at what dies when I leave the promised land, i.e. that place of God's promises!

3. Boaz did not force himself upon Ruth. He was available and waited for her to come to him. Does that compare to how you were won over to Jesus?

SAUL: THE
REQUESTED KING

THE FIRST KING of Israel had many flaws. The serious student of the Bible cannot be faulted in wondering how in the world Saul could be a type of the Lord. Indeed, Saul was a crossover. By that, I mean that along with being a picture of Jesus early in his reign, Saul also typifies the unbelieving portion of Israel as seen later in his life in his many attempts to kill David, the one to whom Saul's anointing had been transferred.

But his Jesus moment came in dealings with men of Jabesh-Gilead. After Samuel had anointed Saul king, but before the people had truly embraced him, Nahash, the king of the Ammonites came against the little town of Jabesh-Gilead (1 Samuel 11). Near the Jordan River but on the east side in the land of Gad, Jabesh-Gilead was sort of an outcast in Israel. In fact, about one hundred years earlier, they were chastised by the rest of the nation when they did not come to the aide of the nation during their dealings with a grievous sin committed by the men of Benjamin (Judges 19–21). Without many options, the men of Jabesh-Gilead asked Nahash to make a covenant with them. The Ammonite king replied that he would spare them but only if the men submitted to one very unpleasant condition. That being, they would allow the Ammonites to thrust out their right eyes! This of course, while sparing their lives, would make them unfit for any future battle. Thus, the elders of the city asked for seven-day respite to consider their two painful options—that of battle with probable death versus life in a permanently darkened and dimmed state. During that time, messengers were sent to Saul to ask for help, not really sure if he could or would. But to the rescue, Saul came! In righteous anger, Saul hewed an ox and sent word to the men of Israel that he would do the same to them if they did not come to Jabesh-Gilead's aid. An army of 330,000 was immediately raised, and almost overnight, they marched the thirty-five miles from Gibeah to Jabesh-Gilead. There, Saul and the men of Israel routed Nahash, and the men of the downtrodden city were saved!

I love this story! Let me tell you why. Nahash is a clear Old Testament picture of Satan. His name means "viper," and as the king of the enemies of God's children, he encamped against them just as Satan will do to you and me. In their fearful surprise at Nahash's appearance outside their walls, they made a bad decision. That is, they asked Nahash to make a covenant or a peace treaty with them. Now you can see that on the spiritual side of this story, in considering who Nahash typifies, that it is never a good idea to ask the devil to make a pact with us! Since we are God's children, he can't destroy us, but he can injure us severely if we allow. He can take us out to such a degree that we are no longer fit for the spiritual battles that rage all the time around us. He can make us irrelevant in our daily lives, not functioning as we desire as children of the king!

So the leaders of Jabesh-Gilead realized that the covenant with Nahash wasn't such a bright idea, so they came to their senses and called upon Saul. They called upon the king. Saul, whose name means "requested," flew upon Nahash in moral indignation and utterly destroyed the viper. That obviously is also what our Lord did! The true requested one went to the cross and utterly destroyed the hold that the serpent has over us. No longer are we unfit for battle. Whenever we sin, rebel, or act cowardly, we can immediately return to the battle. Just look at the stories of Samson, Jonah, and Peter to see this in play. Sampson sinned yet still had the power to take out the Philistines. Jonah rebelled yet still witnessed to Nineveh, and Peter was a coward in denying his Lord yet still was told by Jesus to feed his lambs. Yes, because of Jesus' triumph over the greater than Nahash, we can always have victory also. "For the gifts and calling of God are without repentance" (Romans 11:29). Go for it, dear believer, for the one Saul reveals in this story has freed you from the viper!

For further study:

1. Nahash the viper is a clear picture of Satan in the Bible. Can you think of any other characters in the Old Testament & the gospels who typify our adversary?

2. Have you ever been bloodied & bruised by Satan after compromising with him?

3. Abraham sold-out his wife Sarah on two separate occasions to save his neck while in fear of neighboring leaders, yet God still blessed him. Has God ever blessed you even when you were in the midst of a sin? What does that teach you about our Lord?

DAVID: THE GIANT KILLER

OF ALL OF the Old Testament people who are types of the Messiah, the one most often and most closely associated with Jesus Christ may be Israel's greatest king, David. The Bible devotes many pages, chapters, and even entire books to develop the exploits and thoughts of the one God calls "a man after his own heart." Many of those deeds and devotions of David can be seen and were fulfilled in the person of Jesus of Nazareth.

Fortunately, the distance to Emmaus was seven miles, as it likely took our Lord one of those miles just to speak of his many associations to King David! Let's look at some of the ties. A few I will develop, and many I will only be able to list as entire books could be written on how David is a picture of our Lord.

Every Jew understands that the Messiah is to be the Son of David, that is, the future king would be of the line of David. This is known as the Davidic Covenant, and it was the covenant God made with the king after David asked God if he could build him a house.

> Also the Lord telleth thee that he will make thee an house
> (family tree). And when thy days be fulfilled and thou
> shalt sleep with thy fathers, I will set up thy seed after thee,
> which shall proceed out of thy bowels, and I will establish
> his kingdom…I will be his father and he shall be my son…
> and thine house and thy kingdom shall be established for-
> ever before thee: Thy throne shall be established forever.
>
> 2 Samuel 7:11–16

The fulfillment of this promise is given in the opening verses of Matthew. In that gospel, the one that portrays Jesus' royal ties, we see that Jesus Christ is the twenty-eighth son of King David (Matthew 1:17). That is because in the Old Testament and gospel days, all Jewish men knew of their lineage, tracking all the way back through their father Abraham and even beyond through Heber (where we get the word *Hebrew*) to Noah and ultimately back to Adam (Luke 3:23–38). But after the Romans razed Jerusalem in AD 69–70, all of the lineage records were destroyed! This is important to understand. That is, because since the time shortly after Jesus Christ, no man on the face of this planet can claim to be a direct descendent of King David for the recorded proof is just not available! To the Jews, who are still waiting for their messiah, they can never be sure if that future monarch will fulfill the Davidic covenant as the records are no longer in exist-ence. Except for the one who does have his records and who said to Caiaphas, when the high priest asked him if he were the Christ. "I am [the name for God!]: And ye shall see the Son of man sitting on the right hand of power, and coming in the clouds of heaven" (Luke 14:62).

Because the Messiah is recognized to be the son of David, later in the prophetical writings, those men, when speaking of the Messiah, were free to call the future king, David.

> And they shall serve the Lord their God, and David their
> king, whom I will raise up unto them.
>
> Jeremiah 30:9

And David my servant shall be king over them; and they shall have one shepherd…And my servant David shall be their prince forever.

Ezekiel 37:24–25

Afterward shall the children of Israel return, and seek the Lord their God, and David their king; and shall fear the Lord and his goodness in the latter days.

Hosea 3:5

Sixty three of the psalms from the book with the same name are attributed to David. In many of those poems, David is given inspiration from God to speak of the trials and exploits of his future son as well as himself. We will address many of these predictions when we come to the section of this book called "Prophecies" about Jesus.

David had three anointings as king. The first was a private affair in front of only his family when Samuel anointed the shepherd boy as the spiritual king even while Saul held the secular office as the monarch (1 Samuel 16:3). Later, after Saul's death, David was anointed king over Judah (2 Samuel 2:4). Lastly, David was anointed as king over all of Israel after the deaths of Abner and Ishbosheth (2 Samuel 5:3). Likewise, Jesus is seen having three coronations as king in the book, which fully reveals him as Lord and king, that being the book of Revelation. His first anointing is also only in front of the family as up in heaven we will hear the angels sing with a loud voice, "Worthy is the Lamb that was slain to receive power, and riches, and wisdom, and strength, and honor, and glory, and blessing" (Revelation 5:12). Our Lord's second anointing will be in front of his tribe, if you will, as he will be crowned in front of those redeemed out of the tribulation. That is, like David, Jesus will be recognized by those who had initially refused to acknowledge his kingship.

And the seventh angel sounded; and there were great voices in heaven saying, the kingdoms of this world are

become the kingdoms of our Lord, and of his Christ; and
he shall reign for ever and ever.

Revelation 11:15

Jesus' last coronation will be in front of all, as was David's,
when he returns in flaming fire as King of kings and Lord of lords.

> And I saw heaven opened, and behold a white horse; and
> he that sat upon him was called Faithful and True, and in
> righteousness he doth judge and make war. His eyes were
> a flame of fire, and on his head were many crowns…he
> was clothed in a vesture dipped in blood: And his name
> is called the Word of God. And the armies which were in
> heaven followed him upon white horses, clothed in fine
> linen, white and clean…And he hath on his vesture and
> on his thigh a name written, KING OF KINGS, AND
> LORD OF LORDS.

Revelation 19:11–14, 16

David was a shepherd, the youngest son of Jessie, not who
Samuel expected to be chosen as Israel's anointed (1 Samuel
16:7). Likewise Jesus, who called himself the Good Shepherd
and coming from the backwater town of Nazareth, also did not
appear as one destined to be chosen to ascend to David's throne.
God's words to Samuel bear repeating here.

> Look not on his countenance, or on the height of his
> stature…for the Lord seeth not as a man seeth; for man
> looketh on the outward appearance, but the Lord looketh
> on the heart.

1 Samuel 16:7

David was from Bethlehem as was Jesus. The importance
of this association is underscored by the prophet Micah in his
famous words revealing that the ruler in Israel would come out
of the little town of Bethlehem (Micah 5:2). But this was no
easy task in considering that the Son of David's mother and

earthly father lived in Nazareth, a town forty miles to the north of Bethlehem. God moved the entire Roman Empire in order to get this to happen. You might say the Almighty was showing off! "By coincidence," Caesar Augustus ordered a worldwide taxation of all of the people. Men were required to travel to the home of their ancestry. Thus, in moving the mountain, Jesus was born in Bethlehem!

The leaders of the nation were jealous of both David and of Jesus, and they acted upon their resentment. After David had slaughtered the Philistines, the women of the nation composed a little song, which glorified David over Saul. This led to an evil spirit vexing Saul into a murderous rampage in his efforts to kill David (found in 1 Samuel 18). Just as in the case of David, the devil entered into Judas and undoubtedly inspired Caiaphas and the leaders of the nation to bring Jesus to the destruction they so desperately wanted to be his fate.

David married a woman named Abigail (1 Samuel 25), a woman of good understanding and of a beautiful countenance. Abigail's name means "source of joy," yet she was married to a harsh man named Nabal. As a picture of the law, Nabal was unable to protect Abigail, but as Abigail came to David in humility, she was covered while Nabal subsequently died. In this we see Jesus. When we as Abigail, as the bride, came to Jesus in humility, we too died to the law that Nabal typifies. We too became the bride of Christ! We are taken as Jesus' bride just as Abigail was taken as David's.

Many times David was inspired to sing figuratively of the travails he suffered in the days before he ascended to the throne. All agreed that literal fulfillment of David's songs occurred in the person of his son, Jesus.

> I will declare the decree: The Lord hath said unto me,
> Thou art my Son; this day have I begotten thee.
>
> Psalm 2:7

For thou wilt not leave my soul in hell (*Hades; the grave*); neither wilt thou suffer thine Holy One to see corruption.

Psalm 16:10

All that see me laugh me to scorn: They shoot out the lip, they shake the head saying, He trusted on the Lord that he would deliver him: Let him deliver him, seeing he delighted in him.

Psalm 22:7–8

For dogs have compassed me: The assembly of the wicked have enclosed me: They pierced my hand and feet. I may tell all my bones: They look and stare upon me. They part my garments among them, and cast lots upon my vesture.

Psalm 22:16–18

Because for thy sake I have borne reproach; shame hath covered my face. I am become a stranger unto my brethren, and an alien unto my mother's children. For the zeal of thine house hath eaten me up; and reproaches of them that reproached thee are fallen on me...Reproach hath broken my heart; I am full of heaviness: And I looked for some to take pity, but there was none; and for comforters, but I found none. They gave me gall for my meat; and in my thirst they gave me vinegar to drink.

Psalm 69:7–9, 20–21

Lastly, the story of David and Goliath is the classic story that even the most unschooled in the things of the Bible is familiar. It is a wonderful account that reveals Jesus to all who have eyes to see!

The giant Goliath, whose name means "stripper," was the champion of Israel's enemy, the Philistines. For forty days, he taunted Saul and the men of Israel saying that it was incredulous that in all of the camp of Israel, no one could be found who was brave enough to stand before him in battle. This is what

Satan, the one Goliath typifies, also does. He too, continually has taunted us that we are unworthy and unfit for spiritual battle. As the accuser of the brethren, the devil continually reminds you and me that we are sinners and failures. Then along came David and along came the one David pictures. David declared, "For who is this uncircumcised Philistine that he should defy the armies of the living God?" (1 Samuel 17:26). He then went out against the monster, with all of the eyes of Israel upon him, and felled the warrior in a most unexpected way. He used a shepherd's sling, the weapon used to chase away wolves from the flock, to take down the stripper.

Then David took Goliath's own weapon, his huge sword, and cut off his head. The men of Israel were emboldened by David's heroics and subsequently routed the camp of their enemies. Likewise, this also is what the greater than David, the Son of David, did. He also took on the champion—the enemy of God's people in a most unexpected way. He went to the cross and died, yet in him was found no sin. Thus, the redeemer took the death we all were destined to and, thereby, cancelled our debt. He purchased us back from the clutches of the god of this world. Jesus took the terrible weapon of Satan, the cross, and used it against him. The Lamb of God thus fulfilled the prophecy God revealed to the serpent when the Almighty told Satan that he would bruise the heel of the promised one while the one David models would bruise his head. And just like in that past battle, because of our Lord's victory, now we are emboldened and able to rout the camp of our enemies as we take the spiritual weapons of the word and of the Spirit, effectively engaging in battle against Satan and his minions.

Truly, the story of David and Goliath is an Old Testament account that undoubtedly was part of that Bible study on the road to Emmaus!

Now before we move on to another picture of Christ, I have a thought I would like to consider from David's life. As we first noted, David was promised by God that he would establish his kingdom though his son. And it would be a kingdom that would last forever. Of course, David's son was Solomon, and as we understand, that kingdom did not last forever. Thus, one would conclude that the simplistic understanding of God's words to David was not what God was promising. That's the way it most often is. Things are not always what they appear with God concerning his answers to our prayers as well as his promises to us. But He does answer our prayers, and he does fulfill his promises often though, they are not in ways that our puny little brains could have foreseen! Like the promise to David, they are much bigger than we can imagine. When God says he will never leave us and never forsake us, it doesn't necessarily mean that we won't get in an automobile accident tomorrow or get sick next week. It may mean that, but most likely, it is much bigger than that. Bad things can and will happen, but if and when they do, God will be there to see us through. He will be there to carry us forth. He will keep us from being destroyed and disqualified eternally no matter what!

For further study:

1. David's name means "beloved one." How does that name relate to the greater than David, Jesus Christ?

2. How does the story of David & Goliath relate to Jesus' words when he stated that he was building his church and the gates of hell would not prevail against it?

3. Have you ever misunderstood a promise in God's word to you? Have you seen God's faithfulness even in your misunderstanding yet?

Solomon: Wisdom, Peace, and Majesty

T HE BIBLE DEVOTES many words to David's son, Solomon. Once again, one of the reasons is because King Solomon is a powerful, though less than perfect, picture of Jesus Christ.

Solomon, as the first son of David in the Christ line who reigned as king was the one in that group who most typified our Lord. There were six in all who were kings, making Jesus the seventh. Matthew 1:6–8.

Solomon is noted as being the wisest man in the Old Testament. The poetry of the psalms and proverbs, which Solomon was inspired to write, are an everlasting testament to his gift of wisdom. Solomon received his God-given wisdom because he asked. At the onset of his reign, God appeared to Solomon and told him to request anything he desired. Solomon in his humility did not ask for power, riches, and prestige like so many others would have, but he longed for wisdom and knowledge in order to lead the nation. What a response that was! In answering Solomon's request, God was very pleased. He told the son of David that indeed, he would be the wisest man the world had ever seen and also he was going to pour out all of the other blessings he could have asked for but did not.

Riches and power and fame were thrown in for good measure (2 Chronicles 1:7–12)! As an aside, the Bible also tells us to go to the Father for wisdom. Let me show you.

> If any of you lack wisdom, let him ask of God, that giveth to all men liberally, and upbraideth not; and it shall be given him.
>
> James 1:5

In Jesus, we constantly see his connection to the wisdom of Solomon. In our Lord's dealings with the leaders of the nation, we were continually amazed at his discretion and brilliance! When he said to the men who were accusing the woman caught in adultery "let he who is without sin cast the first stone" (John 8:7), his words stopped them cold. The time Jesus told the priests to render to Caesar the things which belong to Caesar and to render to God the things which belong to God continues to bring a smile to my face whenever I reread that account (Matthew 22:15–22)! The Bible states that in Jesus are hid all of the treasures of wisdom and knowledge (Colossians 2:3). On that day not very far away, the Bible gives a Solomon-like description of Jesus. When we are all together praising him, we will sing with a loud voice, "Worthy is Lamb that was slain to receive power, and riches, and wisdom, and strength, and honor, and glory, and blessing" (Revelation 5:12). Truly Jesus is the only wise God (1 Timothy 1:17)!

Along with wisdom, Solomon shares another bond with our Lord—that of peace and abundance. Solomon's name means "peace" and his reign was typified by its incredible pacifity and wealth. Of course Jesus pronounced peace to his disciples and to the people on numerous occasions (most notably John 16:33), and even the most unschooled in the words of Isaiah know that the redeemer is called the prince of peace (Isaiah 9:6). When we look at Solomon's forty-year reign we see a picture of the Millennial Kingdom of Jesus Christ. In his day, many, including the Queen of Sheba, came to hear the wisdom and see the majesty and abundance of Solomon and his kingdom. Indeed, that day foreshadowed that future era when Christ will reign as King of kings and Lord of lords. Solomon's rule portrayed in the scriptures of the time when the lion will lie down with the lamb and when all will travel yearly to Jerusalem to praise the king and to hear his wisdom (Zechariah 14:16). What a day that will be!

Now before we leave Solomon, we must speak of this type of wisdom, which Solomon and Jesus possess. The Bible personifies wisdom as a woman and implores the sons of God to seek after it. We learn in the Proverbs that we must incline our ears to wisdom and to apply our hearts to understanding (Proverbs 2:2). We must comprehend that it is the Lord who gives wisdom (Proverbs 2:6) and that by wisdom, the way of the saints will be preserved (Proverbs 2:8). We are told that wisdom will deliver the man of God from evil (Proverbs 2:12), and that it is the principal thing far more valuable than all one's earnings (Proverbs 4:7). Most importantly, we remember that the fear of the Lord is the beginning of wisdom (Proverbs 9:10). Obviously, the ascertainment of wisdom is a key to successful living. But I submit to you, that while it is the principal thing, it is not highest thing. Far above wisdom is love. If a man or woman can only have one, we must seek to be lovers over wise guys. In fact, the Bible warns us about gaining wisdom without it's bedfellow of love. In speaking to the Corinthians about their freedom in the Lord, Paul proclaimed, "Knowledge puffeth up, but love edifies" (1 Corinthians 8:1). He points out that too much knowledge can tempt me to not rely on God. To think I can handle my life situations on my own. You may remember the name of the fruit tree that Adam and Eve partook of—the tree of knowledge of good and evil! Indeed, wisdom without love can lead to disaster.

Wisdom without love also amounts to nothing!

> And though I have the gift of prophecy, and understand all mysteries, and all knowledge; and though I have all faith, so that I could remove mountains, and have not love, I am nothing.
>
> I Corinthians 13:2

Jesus spoke an interesting statement I would like to consider in this context of Solomon's wisdom and the need for the counterweight of love. He indicted the Pharisees for their unbelief as he said, "The Queen of the South shall rise up in judgment with this generation, and shall condemn it: For she came from the uttermost parts of the earth to hear the wisdom of Solomon; and behold, a greater than Solomon is here" (Matthew 12:42). In comparing himself to Solomon, Jesus appropriately elevated himself over Israel's most regal sovereign. There are countless reasons he could do that, but the one we are considering in this discussion is our Lord's incredible love! Jesus later displayed a sacrificial love, a dying love, which I cannot comprehend! He loved me while I was dead in my trespasses and sins and went to the cross dying for me so I could live! He did that for you too! What love he showed. What love he lived. Honestly, I don't understand that kind of love. But I thank God for it!

For further study:

1. What was it about Solomon's request for wisdom to lead the children of Israel that pleased God so greatly? How can you apply what you see in Solomon's story in guiding your prayers to the Father?

2. What is your favorite gospel story demonstrating Jesus' keen intellect? How does Jesus exemplify James 1:19 as we examine the wise words we hear from him?

3. Solomon was the son of David & Bathsheba. You may remember that their relationship began in adultery & murder. Why do you suppose Jesus chose to come to this planet as a descendent from such an evil liaison?

Jonah: The Resurrected Prophet

THE RESURRECTION OF Jesus Christ is the pivotal point of human history. As the Apostle Paul pointed out to the Corinthians, who were being influenced by the Epicurean philosophy of their day (a philosophy still very alive in our day too, which says that this life is all there is), "If Christ be not raised, your faith is in vain; ye are yet in your sins...If in this life only we have hope in Christ, we are of all men most miserable" (1 Corinthians 15:15:17, 19)! Without the resurrection, we are all dead. We are without hope. But Christ has risen from the dead, and the Old Testament prophet Jonah was a sneak preview to Israel that the redeemer would also verify his claim as messiah by rising as did Jonah.

> Then certain of the scribes and of the Pharisees answered, saying, Master, we would see a sign from thee [we need

proof that you are who you say you are]. But he answered and said unto them, An evil and adulterous generation seeketh after a sign; and there shall be no sign be given to it, but the sign of Jonah: For as Jonah was three days and three nights in the whale's belly; so shall the Son of man be three days and three nights in the heart of the earth.

Matthew 12:38–40

In Jonah's story, we learned that the prophet was running from the Lord after he was instructed by God to witness to Israel's enemy the Assyrians of Nineveh. The ruler of the earth sent a storm nearly capsizing the boat in which Jonah was traveling. The men of the vessel sensed that their evil was due to circumstances relating to human rebellion and sin, and thus, the passengers were questioned as to the possible reason for their dire situation. Jonah confessed that it was indeed due to his refusal to obey God's command to him that the tempest was upon them. He told them that he needed to die for the others to live. He basically said that the payment for his sin would require his death and that that payment would then spare the rest of his shipmates. We know this to be true as Paul so poignantly pointed out in Romans, "For the wages of sin is death, but the free gift of God is eternal life through Christ Jesus our Lord" (Romans 6:23).

Jonah was tossed overboard and was swallowed up by a great fish, which Jesus affirmed was a whale. Obviously dying, Jonah spent three days and three nights in that aquatic tomb before miraculously being cast out onto a beach and made alive. After that, Jonah did go to Nineveh, and the Bible tells us that the entire city of 600,000 people believed his message and repented. Jesus, in alluding to this story, was telling the scribes and the Pharisees he was telling the skeptics to check out the story of Jonah. See what happened to Jonah if you want proof of who I am and what I'm going to do. Just as Jonah died as payment for sin, so will I. Just as Jonah came back to life after three days and three nights, I will also. And just as the men of fallen Nineveh repented at seeing a dead man risen back to life, so will the men of this evil world repent when they see that I have paid for their sin and conquered death.

Truly, the prophet Jonah was on the lips of our Lord as he spoke to those men on the road to Emmaus as the story of Jonah is a profound illustration of the reality of the resurrection of Jesus Christ!

So what does this story tell you and me? What do I learn that I can use when I deal with the skeptics? That's easy! Don't talk about evolution. Don't discuss whether Jesus is God or just the Son of God. Speak one thing and one thing only. That Jesus died for my sins as did Jonah, that he was entombed for three days and three nights as was Jonah, and that he rose again as did Jonah! Speak that Christ's death, burial, and resurrection is the central belief of life. To embrace him is eternal regeneration, but to reject him is everlasting destruction.

> For I delivered unto you first of all that which I also received, how that Christ died for our sins according to he the scriptures; and that he was buried, and that he rose again according to the scriptures.
>
> 1 Corinthians 15:4

Truly, the resurrection of the Christ was foretold in the scriptures!

For further study:

1. Jonah's name means "dove" and he was immersed in water. How does that relate to Jesus' story?

2. Why is the death, burial & resurrection of Christ such good news?

3. Do you see a problem with Jesus' words to the Pharisees when he said he would be in the heart of the earth for

three days & three nights? How do you resolve this apparent discrepancy with other scriptures teaching that Jesus died on Friday & rose on Sunday? What should you do when you think you see an error in God's word?

ESTHER: SAVIOR TO GOD'S PEOPLE

THE BOOK OF Esther is one of my favorites in all of scripture. In it, the name of God is not found, yet his fingerprints are all over it! The story is layered with multiple allegories. Jesus undoubtedly shared to the men on the road to Emmaus the picture of how the story of Esther declares the account of salvation.

Xerses, whose title was Ahasuerus, a name meaning "Exalted Father" was the absolute ruler of the world at the time. He of course pictures God the Father in our story. He was married to a beautiful and discreet queen named Vashti. In a season prior to battling the Greeks, the king held a feast for all of the warriors of the empire. On the last day of the feast, the king called for Queen Vashti to show off her beauty to the nobles of the kingdom. Vashti refused and was sent away for her rebellion. In our story, this faultless queen typifies the law. For indeed, the law is perfect. It came first, but it cannot save.

Afterward, the king sought another. Many women were brought before Ahasuerus, but none satisfied him until he met Esther. In this part of the narrative, the other women picture the philosophies and false religions of the world, which also are unable to redeem God's people. Esther whose name means "Star" is of course a wonderful type of the bright morning star Jesus Christ! The Bible states that she was fair to look upon i.e. she was beautiful and that she pleased all that knew her. She loved Ahasuerus just as Jesus is so intimately in fellowship with the Almighty.

The story becomes even more interesting as the plot thickens. Tension is introduced when a powerful yet subtle man named Haman comes into conflict with Esther's cousin and former caregiver named Mordecai. Haman was the second in command in the kingdom and can be seen as a picture of Satan and/or the Antichrist (you can take your pick). Mordecai is a type of the Jewish nation, and he also pictures all of God's children in this allegory. Haman hated Mordecai for the latter's refusal to bow down to him just as Satan hates the people of God for our refusal to blindly follow after him. Thus, Haman devised a plan to get a death sentence placed upon all of the people of Mordecai just as the serpent subtly tricked Adam, placing the curse of death upon all of his children also. But when our heroine heard of the plot she came to the rescue. She did the unthinkable! That is, she went before the king without being called.

The significance of this can be missed in the account but is very important. Whenever a person came before the king without being called, certain death awaited. Esther knew this, yet chose to go nonetheless. She said, "So I will go before the king, which is not according to law: And if I perish, I perish" (Esther 4:16). Obviously, this section of the story typifies Christ's actual road to the cross. Like Esther, Christ willingly chose to perish to save his people. Esther went before Ahasuerus and that sovereign held out the golden scepter signifying his acceptance of her self-sacrifice. Then Esther exposed to the king what Haman had plotted against her people just as Jesus intercedes on our behalf from the accusations of the one who Haman typifies. The Jews were now at peace with the king, yet they still had the sentence of death over them. Once again, Esther came to the rescue. She said,

> If it please the king, and if I have found favor in his sight, and the thing seem right before the king, and I be pleasing in his eyes, let it be written to reverse the letters devised by Haman...For how can I endure to see the evil that shall come unto my people?
>
> Esther 8:5–6

Likewise, the greater than Esther also is most pleasing to the Father. He too has reversed the letters devised by Satan. At the end of the story, we learned of a season of rest for God's people known to the Jews as the Feast of Purim. The Bible states it in these beautiful words,

> As the days wherein the Jews rested from their enemies, and the month which was turned unto them from sorrow to joy, and from mourning into a good day.
>
> Esther 9:22

This part of the story of course illustrates the believer's victory over death and speaks of the day when we will live with heaven on earth, that time which is called the millennial kingdom and the new heaven and new earth. That day pictured in the Feast of Purim when we will all live happily ever after!

Yes, what a wonderful story. It could be made into a blockbuster movie. All of the ingredients are present. Best of all, it's true. It's true for you, it's true for me, and it's true for all time!

I can't resist speaking of another allegory found in this story. That is, how Esther pictures you and me as the bride of Christ. Esther was willing to die sacrificially to save others. We too, as Jesus' beautiful bride, should desire to die daily to see others elevated. That is what our Lord meant when he told us to take up our cross daily and follow him.

The Bible tells us that Esther put on her royal apparel as she went before the king as he sat upon his royal throne. Likewise, we are robed in the righteousness of Christ as we go before the Father. Because of our covering, the Bible wonderfully tells us,

> Let us therefore come boldly (freely) unto the throne of grace, that we may obtain mercy (touch the golden scepter), and find grace to help in time of need.
>
> Hebrews 4:16

What a wonderful king we serve. What a wonderful husband we are married too. What a star is the book of Esther!

For further study:

1. Esther's name means "star" as indeed, she was a super-star. But it can also mean "hidden" as in how a star is hidden by the daylight. In that context, scholars have pointed out that besides picturing Christ's ministry of salvation, the book of Esther also portrays the ministry of the Holy Spirit. Do you see that connection as you read the book of Esther?

2. Esther was purified with spices including the oil of myrrh for one year prior to her audience with the king. How is that a picture of our life here on earth prior to meeting our king in the air on that day not very far away?

3. Take up your cross & follow me, he said. Can you think of a time when you sacrificially did that? How did you feel afterwards?

PART 2

PICTURES
TYPIFYING JESUS

NOAH'S ARK: DELIVERED FROM THE WATERS OF DESTRUCTION

NOW WE HAVE come to the second section of this book. In this section, we will examine pictures and types of Jesus found in the Old Testament. We remember that the scholastic term for Jesus typology is called the "Red Thread." Jesus of course isn't a red three-chorded rope, but he is what that rope represented to Rahab and her family, and he is that to you and me also. He is the one who has and will deliver us when the walls of Jericho come tumbling down! He is the Red Thread.

The first picture Jesus may have explained to Cleophas and the other sojourner on the road to Emmaus may have been Noah's Ark. For indeed, that famous ark is a wonderful type of Jesus Christ. Let me show you.

From Genesis 6, we learn that in the first seventeen hundred years of biblical history, the fallen world after Adam had become greatly depraved. God told Noah that he "saw that the wickedness of man was great in the earth and that the imagination of the thoughts of his heart was only evil continually" (Genesis 6:5). God said that it repented him "that he hade made man on the earth, and it grieved him at his heart" (Genesis 6:6). He then said that, "I will destroy man whom I have created from the face of the earth; both man, and beast, and the creeping thing, and the fowls of the air; for it repenteth me that I have made them" (Genesis 6:7).

This was not good for man. Here we learn that even before the law was given, man had cursed himself and would require judgment. We know from the New Testament scriptures that the judgment for sin is death (Romans 6:23). Thus, God was entirely acting within his holy parameters when he told Noah what was about to come down.

But God, being true to his nature (Exodus 34:6) made a way of escape. The merciful one told Noah, "Make thee an ark of gopher wood; rooms shalt thou make in the ark, and shall pitch it within and without with pitch (Genesis 6:14). God said to take gopher wood, the wood used to make coffins and build an ark. The Bible subsequently gives the dimensions of the ark. It was longer than a football field. Sort of like something you might find today in the Royal Caribbean fleet! Noah was to pitch the ark with pitch. In English, the meaning of this is lost, but in Hebrew, the word for the sticky substance that keeps a boat from taking in water and the word for the payment for a wrongdoing are one and the same. That is, the word for *pitch* and the word for *atonement* are alike. Indeed, just as the pitch kept the waters of destruction from taking down the ark, so too Jesus' sacrifice keep the waters of our sin and depravity from sinking you and me!

So Noah built the ark, and when it was finished, God told Noah to take his family and two of all animals into the ark where they were safely ensconced away from the forty days of relentless worldwide rain. All flesh was judged and destroyed while those on the ark were safely delivered. Of course, this is the picture of Jesus. We too are all under the curse of sin and the judgment of death, which that curse requires. But we who have come to Jesus, the ship of salvation, are and will be carried safely over the waters of destruction while those not onboard will unfortunately be without a lifeboat.

It's also interesting to me that the ark was to have only one door. That makes sense, doesn't it? Jesus is the way, the truth, and the life. He is the door. There is only one way into the ship of salvation. Only one door. It's the Lord!

Now before we proceed to the next picture of the Savior that Jesus may have opened up to the two men, there is a nagging question one may have from this discussion. That is, how can God judge the sin of man *before* he had given the law? For it is the law that Paul said in Galatians is our schoolmaster to lead us to Christ (Galatians 3:24). It is the law that reveals to us that we need a Savior. Well, the answer to this dilemma is found in the book of Romans.

In the first three chapters, we learn that man is indicted by the commandments of God in chapter three, but we read in chapters one and two that all of creation and man's inherent conscious also cry against us that we are without excuse. We know this to be true, don't we? Every nation, every tribe, every tongue understands that there is a God, and we innately know what is right and what is wrong. We don't learn that it is wrong to kill and steal. We are born knowing that! Now it may be another thing when man chooses not to do what he knows is right. That's where we come to sin. All men are cursed as we continually do what we know is wrong. That's the message of Romans 1 and 2.

All of creation and all of our consciousness reveal that there is a God and that we fall woefully short of his standards. The revealed word correctly points out that we are in deep trouble, and indeed, we need a redeemer! Thus, because of chapters 1 and 2, because of God's work of creation and because of the conscience within, we all know that we are sinners under the righteous judgment of the Almighty. Thank God for his Son. For without him, we are down the creek without a paddle. We are out on the ocean without an ark!

For further study:

1. Noah's ark pictures Christ's ministry of salvation from destruction. Can you think of any other water-born vessels in the Bible which also portray this type?

2. Jesus said, "As the days of Noah were, so shall also the coming of the Son of man be" (Matthew 24:37). How are the days in which we live today like the days of Noah found in Genesis 6?

3. Do you think Paul was correct when he affirmed that all are born with a conscience discerning right from wrong (Romans 2:12-15)? What do you think he meant when he said that in the latter times some would depart from the faith having their conscience seared (1 Timothy 4:1-2)? What does a seared conscience look like?

UNDER THE TREE: SUBMITTED TO HIS SACRIFICE

THE PEOPLE OF the biblical world venerated the tree, that most majestic of plants. Thus, in the Bible, the tree is used in numerous types and allegories. Beginning in the Garden of Eden, where we are introduced to the tree of life and the tree of the knowledge of good and evil and continuing to the new heaven and new earth, where we partake of the twelve fruited tree of life planted next to the river of life, the tree is a most important symbol of biblical truth. Among many figures, the tree can speak of people and of nations. We note that when our Lord taught that a tree is known by its fruit that he was talking about men in that parable (Matthew 12:33). We remember that when the prophets spoke of the fig tree, the olive tree and the other trees that they were speaking of Israel and the nations (Judges 9:6–15, Hosea 9:10, Joel 1 and 2). But the type that Jesus may have spoken of in his traveling Bible study on that memorable road may have been how the tree can be a picture of the cross of Calvary and of the protective covering that his sacrifice provides to you and me.

There a few examples that comes to mind that the teacher may have included.

First, in Genesis 18, the Lord appeared to Abraham in the heat of the day to tell him that Sarah would have a son in her old age. The place where God communed with Abraham was "under the tree" (Genesis 18:4 and 8). This of course speaks of where we in the New Testament commune with the Lord. It's under the tree. It's at the cross. It's remembering the sacrifice that he made for us as we take communion that we, like Abraham, get the vision that God has for our lives.

The second usage that I think of is at the waters of Marah. In the Exodus account, the people had traveled without water for three days. They were hot and thirsty. Then they came to Marah. In English, Marah means "bitterness." The children came to a bitter place. Has that ever happened to you after three days of heat and thirst? But look at what the Father did for his kids.

> And when they came to Marah they could not drink of the waters…for they were bitter…And the people murmured against Moses, saying, What shall we drink? And he cried to the Lord; and the Lord showed him a tree, which when he had cast into the waters, the waters were made sweet.
>
> Exodus 15:23–25

When the tree was cast into the waters, they were made fresh and drinkable. That of course is what Jesus' sacrifice does also. As we come to the cross, as we remember our Lord's death and resurrection, we lose the bitterness and thirst of our day-to-day worldly grind. The dials are set back, the blinders are removed, and the weight is lifted. It's the cross that makes life sweet!

The next example I think of comes from the book of Judges. When we are introduced to Deborah, that wonderful judge of Israel, we immediately learn something significant about her.

> And she dwelt under the palm tree...between Ramah and Bethel...and the children of Israel came up to her for judgment.
>
> Judges 4:5

Deborah served the people under the palm tree between Ramah and Bethel. Ramah means "high ground," and Bethel of course means "house of God. The picture this reveals is that if one is wanting to serve God's people like Deborah did, as a leader and an overseer, that man or woman must be in that elevated place while staying close to the house of God and residing constantly under the cross, staying under the authority of the Lord. Once again, the tree is a picture of the importance of remembering Jesus' sacrifice.

The last example I think of comes from the life of Elisha. In the book of the kings of Israel, we find a little vignette with much imagery revealing Jesus and the cross. Paraphrasing the story from 2 Kings 6:1–7, we find that the spirit-filled students of the prophet Elisha asked that man of God if they could build a learning center for their studies under him. They wanted to build it on the cool banks of the Jordan River. They asked Elisha to come along, to which the teacher gladly agreed. During the building process, one of the students lost his axe handle as he was chopping wood. The iron handle flew into the river and was apparently lost. Since the student had borrowed the axe from another, he was especially distraught. Seeing this, Elisha asked the young man to show him the place where he lost his cutting instrument. There Elisha took a stick and cast it into the waters. Miraculously, the iron axe handle floated to the surface, and the young prophet reached out and retrieved his iron blade.

Like one of the parables from the gospels, this story is full of types. Elisha, of course is a picture of the Lord. He is the teacher. He is the master. The students typify the spirit-filled believers. We too, long to study under our master in the cool of the day. The axe handle pictures the Holy Spirit within. As we cut away, sometimes we lose our edge. Getting the spirit back? Well, look at the story. The student cried to Elisha who then told him to go to the place where he had lost his power. Casting in a stick, the axe miraculously returned to the young man as he reached out for it.

Likewise, as we cry to Jesus and return to the place where we lost that spirit-filled power in our lives and importantly as we plead the blood of the cross that the stick represents, we too will be able to reach out and take back that spiritual power that our Lord has given us.

The application to the tree is huge. It's the Lamb of God's sacrifice that gives us vision in life. That sacrifice will make all things new. The bitterness of our days can and will be sweet. As we serve others, we will be effective as we stay submitted to our Savior, and lastly, when we find ourselves in a backslidden place, if we return to that place where we were when we were on fire for the Lord, pleading the blood of the cross, we will retrieve that power he has placed within.

For further study:

1. How does the sacrament of communion transport you to the foot of the cross? Do you find yourself meeting with God, like Abraham did, when you celebrate communion?

2. How does 1 John 1:9 tie into the idea of coming to the cross to retrieve the spirit-filled power for ministry?

3. In David's son Absalom's story, he was hung in a tree as he caught his long hair in some branches. How does his story relate to what happened to our Lord on the tree?

JACOB'S LADDER: STAIRWAY TO HEAVEN

THE PATRIARCH JACOB was on the run. He had just stolen the blessing that was reserved for the oldest son, his elder brother Esau, by tricking his father Isaac. Esau was gunning for him, and Jacob knew it. So to keep the boys apart while Esau cooled down, Rebekah, the twins' mother, suggested to Isaac that Jacob travel to the land of their kindred to find a wife. Thus, leaving Beersheba in southern Israel, Jacob traveled north along the road to Pandanaram (Mesopotamia). The first night he stopped in the central highlands of Israel. It was cold and dark, and Jacob must have feared a bit of how things would go as he was alone and still needed to travel hundreds of miles to reach his destination. He laid down to sleep using stones for his pillows, then something wonderful and unexpected occurred.

> And he dreamed, and behold a ladder set up on the earth, and the top of it reached to heaven: And behold the angels of God ascending and descending on it. And behold, the Lord stood above it, and said, I am the Lord God of Abraham thy father, and the God of Isaac: The land whereon thou liest, to thee will I give it, and to thy seed... And, behold, I am with thee in all places whither thou goest...for I will not leave thee. And Jacob awaked out of his sleep, and he said, Surely the Lord is in this place: and I knew it not...this is none other but the house of God (Bethel), and this is the gate of heaven.
>
> Genesis 28:12–13, 15–17

Jacob had his first encounter with the God of Abraham and Isaac, with the God of the universe, with the God who at that point became the God of Jacob! In this type, we are considering, Jacob was "born again." He was now starting a new life with God, leaving his old life of trickery and sin and traveling to a new destination with his Savior.

The ladder of course, is the picture of the redeemer himself. He is the one that spans the gulf between earth and heaven, between sinful man and a holy God. Jacob's ladder is the stairway to heaven. And like that ladder, Jesus is the way, the only way for man to bridge the chasm that separates us from God. Good works won't do it. Much study can't save. Loving people and giving generously in and of itself can't clear the slate. There is only one way—Jacob's ladder!

Some may say, well, that's sort of restrictive. Not really, for if God were to set up many stairways to heaven, then our adversary, Satan, could confuse us even more by setting up many more false paths to God. This way, it's crystal clear. One way, no doubts, no questions, no debate. "I am the way, the truth, and the life: No man cometh unto the Father, but by me (John 14:6).

In the New Testament, this picture of Jesus as Jacob's ladder comes up again. From John 1: 43–51, we read of Jesus calling Philip and Nathaniel to follow him. Nathaniel, who pictures the believing remnant of Israel, initially questioned the wisdom of following a rabbi from the podunk town of Nazareth, saying "Can there any good come out of Nazareth" (verse 46). As a student of the scriptures, Nathaniel rightly asked that question knowing that the Messiah would come from Bethlehem as Micah had previously prophesied. Nonetheless, Nathaniel came with Philip to Jesus and the prophet greeted Nathaniel in a manner that suggested that he knew him well. To that, Nathaniel said, "Whence knowest thou me? Jesus answered…Before that Philip called thee, when thou wast under the fig tree, I saw thee" (verse 48). Sitting under the fig tree is a way of complementing Nathaniel. It denotes an Israelite who is governed by God. Thus, Nathaniel quickly perceived that Jesus was not just an ordinary man, and he praised our Lord. He said, "Rabbi, thou art the Son of God; thou art the King of Israel" (verse 49). To that, Jesus responded stating that hearing him prophecy will fail in comparison to actually seeing heaven opened. He then invoked the imagery of Jacob's ladder to speak of himself.

> And he saith unto him, Verily, verily, I say unto you, Hereafter ye shall see heaven open, and angels of God ascending and descending upon the Son of man.
>
> John 1:51

Jesus on the road to Emmaus certainly spoke of the patriarch Jacob and his famous dream to those two men as they traveled forth.

As an extension of this story, I think of the day when we too will see heaven opened, when we will see the angels ascending and descending upon the Son of man just as Jacob did and just as Nathaniel will. It will be on that day when we hear the shout, the voice, and the trump calling us up to meet the Lord in the air!

After this I looked, and, behold, a door was opened in heaven: And the first voice which I heard was as it were a trumpet talking with me; which said, Come up hither...

Revelation 4:1

For further study:

1. In bible days, the oldest son was the one who received the father's blessing and double portion. Yet in Isaac & Jacob we see the younger son being the blessed one. Why do you think God chose Isaac & Jacob over Ishmael & Esau?

2. Jacob was in the house of God (Bethel), in his presence, yet knew it not. So God spoke to him in a dream. Have you ever heard from the Lord in a dream (Acts 2:17)?

3. Is obeying the Ten Commandments a false stairway to heaven? Why?

Manna: Bread from Heaven

> I am the bread which came down from heaven…I am the
> true bread which came down from heaven: If any man eat
> of this bread, he shall live forever.
>
> John 6:4–5

THE BREAD WHICH came down from heaven was
called manna, and it was given to the children of Israel for forty
years during their wilderness wanderings. Of course, Jesus spoke
of the ties that He and the bread from heaven share on the seven-
mile walk from Jerusalem to Emmaus.

In Exodus 16, we find the account of Jehovah's gift. Israel had
been liberated from Egypt for only one month. They were now at
the sixth camp on their way to Mount Sinai, where God would
proclaim to them the Ten Commandments. It was hot, and they

were tired and hungry. In their weakened state, they had memory blackout and complained to Moses that they missed all of the good food they had back in Egypt. Somehow, they forgot that they were brutally mistreated and in bondage to their Egyptian taskmasters. This complaining didn't upset God though. After all, they were just children. They had only been free for a month. They really didn't know the heart of their God at this point.

That was about to change. Jehovah-jireh, God our provider, was going to show them something of his graciousness. God appeared to all of the people in a cloud of glory and proclaimed that in the morning, he would rain bread from heaven. Sure enough, the next day, little round flecks of food covered the ground around their camp. The children called it *manna*, which means "what is it!" It was round like a coriander seen and appeared as hoar frost upon the ground. Its color was snow white, and it tasted like wafers made with honey. Truly it was delicious! Gods kids gathered it up, and their growling stomachs were filled!

Let's consider how our Lord tied himself to the manna from heaven as he walked with those two privileged men on the road to Emmaus.

Manna came quietly at night just as Emmanuel came to the world on that *silent night* just over two thousand years ago. Manna was given to the children of Israel while they were in the wilderness. Likewise, Jesus left heaven, a land of abundance and beauty to feed us in this fallen and dry land in which we live. Manna came on the dew. It didn't really touch the ground. In like similitude, Jesus became like us but was also different.

Both God and Man, Jesus sort of hovered above the ground, if you will, as always being led by the Spirit, he stayed uncontaminated by the world. Also, in his birth, we see a huge distinction as the bread from heaven was born of a virgin! The Bible states that manna was small, round, white, and tasted like honey wafers. These four descriptions speak of our Lord's humility, eternalness, holiness, and his sweetness.

Most importantly, as noted above, Jesus told his disciples on the night before he was crucified that he is the living bread who came down from heaven. And by eating the bread of his body, one would live forever! Dear reader, give the Lord's table honor. Give communion worth!

For further study:

1. Over time the children grew tired of manna and lusted after meat. In your walk with the Lord has that ever happened to you? Like the backsliding Israelites, did gorging on the meat of the world satisfy you?

2. Manna was to be gathered in the morning while it was fresh. Do you see an application concerning your relationship with Jesus? Is the morning a good time for you to seek him?

3. Jesus is called the word of God. Can you think of any ties between manna and God's word?

THE ROCK: THAT ROCK WAS CHRIST

EVERY GOOD JEW knew that their scriptures spoke of God as a rock—as the rock. On the road to Emmaus, our Lord certainly made the connection of the rock to himself. Let's look at what the word says,

> For who is God, save the Lord? And who is a rock save our God? The Lord liveth; and blessed be my rock; and exalted be the God of the rock of my salvation.
>
> 2 Samuel 22:32, 47

> The Lord is my rock and my fortress, and my deliverer; my God, my strength, in whom I will trust.
>
> Psalm 18:2

> Bow down thine ear to me; deliver me speedily: Be thou
> my strong rock, for an house of defense to save me. For
> thou art my rock and my fortress.
>
> Psalm 31:2–3

> He brought me up also out of an horrible pit, out of the
> miry clay, and set my feet upon a rock...
>
> Psalm 40:2

> Behold a king shall reign in righteousness...And a man
> shall be as an hiding place from the wind, and a covert
> from the tempest; as rivers of water in a dry place, as the
> shadow of a great rock in a weary land.
>
> Isaiah 32:1–2

So we see God as the rock of our salvation very clearly in scripture. But on that wonderful road, Jesus mentioned the two stories of the place called Meribah. For Meribah clearly reveals Jesus as the rock of our salvation just as is the Father!

Found in Exodus 17 and Numbers 20 are the accounts. After their deliverance from the bondage of Egypt, God was leading the children of Israel to Mount Sinai, where he intended to give them the Ten Commandments. On their last stop before reaching the holy mount, the children found themselves in a dry and dusty place. Not yet understanding the faithfulness of their God, they murmured to Moses about their thirsty circumstances. Moses understood God's heart, and instead of murmuring himself, he cried to the Lord. God quenched their thirst in the same way he graciously relieves ours with the rock!

> And the Lord said to Moses, Go on before the people, and
> take with thee the elders of Israel; and thy rod, wherewith
> thou smotest the river, take in thine hand, and go. Behold,
> I will stand before thee there upon the rock in Horeb: and
> thou shalt smite the rock, and there shall come water out
> of it, that the people may drink.
>
> Exodus 17:5–6

Several years later, after the men of Israel again found themselves in a similar bind. Moses again called upon the Lord, and the rock once again gushed forth water (Numbers 20:1–11).

This is what the rock of our salvation did for us, didn't he? Jesus was that rock that was smitten on the cross of Calvary for our murmurings and sins. And because he was smitten, we received the living water, for it is the water which he gives which will cause us to never thirst again!

> Jesus answered and said unto her, Whosoever drinketh of this water shall thirst again: But whosoever drinketh of the water that I shall give him shall never thirst; but the water that I shall give him shall be in him a well of water springing up into everlasting life.
>
> John 4:13–14

> In the last day, that great day of the feast [the last day of the Feast of Tabernacles commemorated the water gushing out of the rock], Jesus stood and cried, saying, if any man thirst, let him come unto me, and drink. He that believeth on me, as the scripture hath said, out of his belly shall flow rivers of living water. [But this he speak of the Spirit, which they that believe on him should receive.]
>
> John 7:37–39

Jesus defined clearly that he was the rock, and the Spirit is the water. How cool is that!

Later, Paul learned of this connection and wrote about it for us in one of his epistles.

> And did all drink the same spiritual drink: For they drank of that spiritual rock that followed them: And that rock was Christ.
>
> 1 Corinthians 10:4

Now before we leave the story of the rock, which gushed forth water, there was another rock found in the Old Testament that also spoke of our Lord. It was called the chief cornerstone, the stumbling stone, the rock of offense, and the stone which the builders rejected; for unfortunately, Jesus is also that rock for those who choose not to believe.

> The stone which the builders rejected is become the cornerstone. This is the Lord's doing; it is marvelous in our eyes.
>
> Psalm 118:22–23

> And he beheld them, and said, What is it then which is written, The stone which the builders rejected, the same is become the head of the corner? Whosoever shall fall upon that stone shall be broken; but on whomsoever it shall fall, it will grind him to powder.
>
> Luke 20:17–18

Truly, our God is a consuming fire! He is not only gentle Jesus, the rock that was smitten, but he is also the chief cornerstone—the rock which will grind to powder all who are not broken up over what he did for them in dying for their sins!

Lastly, the book of Daniel concludes our discussion of Jesus as the rock. In considering the future, we will one day witness the rock of our salvation subdue all of the carnal kingdoms of the world.

> And in the days of these kings shall the God of heaven set up a kingdom, which shall never be destroyed...but it shall break into pieces and consume all these kingdoms, and it shall stand forever. Forasmuch as thou sawest that the stone was cut out of the mountain without hands, and it break into pieces [the former kingdoms]; the great God hath made known unto the king [Nebuchadnezzar] what shall come to pass hereafter.
>
> Daniel 2:44–45

Praise God! We can live for heaven knowing that someday, we will have heaven on earth. On that day, not far away, when the King of kings and the Lord of lords comes back and claims his rightful place on the throne of David. Oh, what a day that will be!

For further study:

1. Psalm 18:2 states that the Lord is my rock and my fortress. Have you ever run to him for strength & protection when there was no where else to go?

2. In Exodus 17 Moses smote the rock. What did that action typify concerning Jesus, the rock? Later Moses was told to speak to the rock in Numbers 20 but instead he again smote the rock. Do you recall what happened to Moses when he smote the rock a second time? Why did that happen to him?

3. Are the concepts of Christ being the head of the body and the cornerstone of the temple related? See Ephesians 2:19-22 for illumination.

Passover: Covered by the Blood of a Lamb

I T WAS THREE days after the Passover celebration when our Lord walked the road to Emmaus. Fresh in their minds was the murder of their teacher at the hands of the Jews. Without a doubt, Jesus would have pointed to the Passover sacrifice and of its perfect fulfillment three days earlier.

> In the tenth day of this month they shall take to them every man a lamb, according to the house of their fathers, a lamb for a house...your lamb shall be without blemish, a male...you shall keep it up until the fourteenth day of the same month: And the whole assembly of the congregation of Israel shall kill it in the evening. And they shall take the blood, and strike it on the...door post of the houses... For I will pass through the land of Egypt this night, and will smite all the firstborn of the land...and against all of the gods of Egypt I will execute judgment: I am the Lord.

> And the blood shall be to you for a token upon the houses
> where you are: And when I see the blood, I will pass over
> you, and the plague shall not be upon you to destroy you,
> when I smite the land of Egypt.
>
> Exodus 12:3, 5–7, 12–13

Later, the Jews were instructed to kill the Passover lamb outside the camp on the north side of the tabernacle. Of course Calvary, where Jesus was crucified was outside of the city to the north! On that fateful last week of our Lord's life, the priests inspected the lamb, if you will, by examining him with questions designed to trip him up (Matthew 22:15–46). Each time the one John the Baptist called the Lamb of God responded with brilliance and wit, revealing to all that he truly was without spot or blemish.

Paul declared the prophetic fulfillment of our Lord's sacrifice most clearly. "For even Christ our Passover is sacrificed for us" (1 Corinthians 5:7).

Wonderfully, in our day today, we get to partake of the Passover lamb every time we celebrate communion with him at his blessed table of bread and wine.

For further study:

1. Paul stated that Jesus fulfilled the Passover. Do you take that literally or figuratively? We saw from the law that the lamb was selected on the tenth day of the month. In the passion story of Christ, what event do you think correlated in Jesus' last week with the Passover lamb being selected on the tenth of Nissan?

2. Moses instructed that the Passover lamb was to be killed on the fourteenth day of the month. Did that day always fall on a Friday? Do you think Jesus was killed on a Friday? Why or why not?

3. The blood of the lamb on the doorposts of the people caused the Angel of Death to passover the children of Israel. How is that like Jesus' sacrifice?

THE SACRIFICES TO THE LORD: RESPONSE TO HIS GRACE AND PAYMENT FOR OUR SINS

AT MOUNT SINAI, after God gave the law found in the book of Exodus, we come to the instructions the Almighty gave to his priests. They were the Levites as the tribe of Levi was chosen for this ministry. The book of course is called Leviticus. In God's eyes, sin is serious and not to be dismissed, thus, Leviticus is a bloody book as it deals with sin. God recognized that his people would not be able to obey the law, which he had given them; therefore, his priests needed to have a way to intercede for the people. The book of Leviticus opens with five sacrifices that were to be offered to the Lord not only as payment for their sins, but also in response to the grace that God displayed in forgiving their sins in the first place! But in addition to these two facets of the sacrifices, they also beautifully point to Jesus the final sacrifice for sin and the ultimate manifestation of God's grace in forgiving our sins. Certainly, Jesus spoke of the Levitical sacrifices as he walked with those men on the road to Emmaus.

The first sacrifice was called the *burnt offering* found in Leviticus 1. It was a voluntary sacrifice and spoke of Christ's total dedication in offering up his life for the sins of man. It could be a bull, goat, lamb, turtledove, or pigeon. It had to unblemished, and if a goat or a lamb, it must be male. The priest was to offer it over wood in fire, and it was to be totally consumed. The feet of the animal was to be washed in water, and the animal was to be flayed open but not divided i.e. not have it bones broken. Significantly, in the case of a goat or lamb, it was to be offered north of the altar. Finally, the Bible tells us that this sacrifice was a sweet savor to the Lord.

In this, we see Jesus Christ, don't we? The suffering servant asked the Father on that dark night in the Garden of Gethsemane if there was any other way. When told there was not, our Lord voluntarily proceeded forward. John the Baptist called Jesus "the lamb of God," prophesying of his fulfillment of this and the other sacrifices. The wood and the fire of course speak of the cross of Calvary and the fire of God's wrath. Our Lord was totally consumed on that day when he redeemed us. The water over the feet pictured his perfect walk. He was naked and pierced for all to see, but none of his bones were broken, and finally our Lord was sacrificed north of the altar just as Calvary is indeed north of the temple!

The second offering was called the *meal offering* found in chapter 2. This also was a voluntary sacrifice, which speaks of Christ's absolute perfection. The meal offering was to be made of fine (sifted) flour or dried corn. It was made delicious by baking or frying with oil, frankincense, and salt. Importantly, no leaven or honey was allowed to be part of this sacrifice. Wonderfully, again, we see Jesus. He was sifted like flour and dried like corn in that he was tempted as are we yet without sin. Oil, speaking of the Holy Spirit, reminds us that indeed, our Lord was given the Spirit without measure.

Frankincense in the Bible speaks of intercessory prayer ascending to God and confirms Jesus' present role at the right hand of the Father where he intercedes for us day and night! Salt of course cleanses and adds flavor and pictures our Lord in that way. Leaven, as a biblical type of sin, was not allowed as Jesus of course was without sin, but why not honey? Honey is sweet and adds flavor as does our Savior, but honey breaks down when heated. The meal offering was heated as was our Lord. He did not break down or give in. He did not come off the cross when they taunted him to do so. Honey would break down and thus could not be part of the wonderful meal offering, picturing our Lord's beauty, flavor, and perfection!

In chapter 3, we learn of the *peace offering*. This was a voluntary celebratory offering in that the one offering the sacrifice as well as the priests would get to partake of the meat of this sacrifice. The peace offering portrays our peace and satisfaction as we celebrate our salvation in Christ. This offering could be of cattle, sheep, or goats. Once again, the sacrifice was to be unblemished and was to be placed over wood and burnt with fire. This time, it could be either male or female, and the fat was to be given to the Lord while the rest of the meat was to be freely eaten by the people. In addition to many of the aspects we saw with the burnt offering, in this sacrifice, we see our Lord in his masculine and feminine side. He was able to turn over the money changer's tables in the temple yet so warm and vibrant that the little children wanted to be with him. The sharing of this sacrifice with the people reminds of those two days when our Lord multiplied the loaves and fish to feed the multitudes. Of course, on the future day, all of his followers will feast at that great banquet found Revelation 19 speaking of the marriage feast of the lamb.

In chapter 4, we come to the first of two mandatory offerings. That is because these two deal with payment for sin instead of our response to God's grace as do the first three. The first sacrifice was called the *sin offering*. It was offered for the general sins of the nation, the priests, the rulers, or the common citizen. The sin offering deals with the sin nature of man. This offering was to be killed before the tabernacle, and the blood of the animal was to be sprinkled upon the altar. The sacrifice would then be burnt outside of the camp where it was totally consumed. The animals to be sacrificed varied according to the station of the sinner. Priests were to offer a young bullock. This was also the requirement to cover the general sins of the nation. Interestingly, the ruler need only offer a male goat or lamb, and a common citizen was only required to offer the same, but in his case, the goat or lamb could be of either gender.

The difference in the offerings suggest that in God's economy, there were differing levels of disobedience depending upon the position and talents the Lord bestows upon a person. A priest would be held to a higher standard as he has been walking with God. This is sobering to me as I remember that Peter told us that we believers in Jesus are a royal priesthood! We are both kings and priests and are held to a higher standard than one who does not know the redeemer. Thankfully, Jesus is the fulfillment of this sacrifice. Jesus as the bullock and the goat and the lamb was consumed once and for all so that our sin nature can and is covered by the blood of his sacrifice!

The last offering our Lord certainly spoke of on the road to Emmaus was called the *trespass offering* found in chapter 5. This offering brought restoration to the sinner for his specific sins. The offering itself is very similar to the sin offering, but its role was quite different. You see, we're not sinners because we sin; no, we sin because we were all born sinners! Thus, the sin offering covers our sin nature, while the trespass offering cleanses us of our specific sins. Jesus did that for us also! He died for the sins of the whole world, but he also died for yours and my specific sins.

When I lie, cheat, and covet, the redeemer became the trespass offering and paid my debt! What a Savior he is!

Therefore, my response to such grace is to be obedient to his commands. For the law given in Exodus 20 was before the sacrifices just as obedience is greater than sacrifice. After Saul disobeyed the command of the Lord, listen to what the prophet Samuel said,

> Hath the Lord as great delight in burnt offerings and sacrifices as in obeying the voice of the Lord? Behold, to obey is better than sacrifice, and to hearken better than the fat of rams.
>
> 1 Samuel 15:22

In fact, throughout God's Word, the student of the scriptures will note that God will not accept the sacrifice of the one whose heart is not right toward him. Sacrifice without godly remorse will accomplish nothing.

So in light of this when we come to the New Testament, we see something very interesting in regards to our sacrificial response to God's grace.

> I beseech you therefore, brethren, by the mercies of God, that ye present your bodies a living sacrifice, holy, acceptable unto God, which is your reasonable service.
>
> Romans 12:1

Unlike the sacrifices of old, we are to be living sacrifices. We are alive and not dead. If we choose, we can come down off of the altar. How do we remain on the altar and acceptable to God? The verse tells us the answer. We are to be holy! Holiness is the key! Holiness equals happiness.

> And be not conformed to this world: But be ye transformed by the renewing of your mind, that ye may prove what is that good, and acceptable, and perfect, will of God.
>
> Romans 12:2

As has been said and written of, the battlefield is in the mind. As I choose to renew my mind, as I choose to put on the mind of Christ, as I choose to walk in the Spirit, I am pleasing and acceptable to the Lord. Being holy by renewing my mind is my reasonable response to God's wonderful matchless grace, which he has shown unto me!

For further study:

1. Once per year, on the Day of Atonement, a goat called the scapegoat was offered for the sins of the people while a second goat was sent out into the desert depicting how the sins of the people were sent away. What type of sacrifice was the scapegoat?

2. Why was the peace offering, portraying the peace & satisfaction we have in Christ a type of the Lord's Table?

3. Why were the sacrifices so bloody? How does that make you feel about sin?

THE TABERNACLE AND IT'S FURNITURE: HE DWELT AMONG US

GOD TOLD MOSES that he desired for the children of Israel to erect a tent called a tabernacle, where he would meet with them. The description of this tent and its furniture give a subtle yet beautiful picture of Jesus Christ. Let me show you some of the nuances from a section of scripture that many have overlooked as detailed and boring, not pertaining to our lives today. Yet, putting on our spiritual glasses will reveal a picture that is anything but dry and dreary.

> And the Lord spake unto Moses, saying, Speak unto the children of Israel...let them make me a sanctuary that I may dwell among them. According to all that I show thee, after the pattern of the tabernacle...even so shall ye make it.
>
> Exodus 25:1–2, 8–9

From the very get-go of this section, God tells his people the purpose he has for the tabernacle. It's a meeting place where the Holy God can meet with us "not so holy" humans.

That's what the Son of God does too, doesn't he? He has bridged the chasm between God and man so that we too can come into the presence of the Holy God.

Look at the opening words from the wonderful gospel of John,

> In the beginning was the Word, and the Word was with God, and the Word was God...All things were made by him...In him was life; and the life was the light of men... And the Word was made flesh, and dwelt among us.
>
> John 1:1, 3–4, 14

Jesus, the word, was made flesh, and the Bible tells us that he dwelt among us. In Greek, the word *dwelt* literally means "tabernacle." Jesus tabernacled. He moved in with us, he became one of us!

So we see from this that the tabernacle and Jesus are related. Let's go back now to Exodus and see some of the details.

> And they shall make an ark of shittim [Acacia] wood... and thou shall overlay it with pure gold...and thou shalt put into the ark the testimony [the Ten Commandments] which I shall give thee...and thou shalt make a mercy seat of pure gold...and thou shall make two cherubims of gold...in the two ends of the mercy seat...and their faces shall look one to another...and thou shalt put the mercy seat above the ark...and there will I meet with thee, and I will commune with thee from above the mercy seat.
>
> Exodus 25:10–22 (excerpts)

The awesome ark of the covenant was the first thing that God told Moses to build. Even before erecting the tent, God wanted to speak of the ark and its mercy seat. You see, before you or I do anything, before we can accomplish anything in life, we need to start with the presence of God. Paraphrasing what Jesus said in John 15:5, I am the vine, and you are the branches. Without me, you can do nothing! And we need his mercy. So it is fitting that the ark is the first detailed instruction given to Moses in this building project picturing Jesus.

We see that the ark was to be made of acacia wood. This substance, which thrives in dry desert climates, is a hard bent wood, which when pierced, emits a resin used to this day as a healing balm. It is not hard to see some spiritual types in this—Isaiah 53 tells us that Jesus came as a root out of dry ground. He was pierced for our transgressions, for our healing. He was earthy; he was human as seen in the acacia wood.

But the wood was also overlaid with gold. This of course, speaks of the heavenly side of our Savior. So we see in the wood and the gold, the earthy and the heavenly, man and God. Jesus, the God man!

Wonderfully, the testimony of the Lord, the Ten Commandments, were to be placed inside the ark. Then they were to be covered by the mercy seat. This is the way it must be. Mercy must triumph over judgment. Jesus said that we must learn mercy. Without mercy, we are doomed as we cannot keep the law! That's why God told Moses to cover the ark with mercy. He showed what he was planning to do. He was going to cover judgment with mercy. "For God so loved the world that he gave his only begotten son that whosoever believeth in him shall not perish, but have eternal life" (John 3:16).

Lastly, before we leave the ark, we see that two angels were at each end of the mercy seat, facing one another. This brings to my mind the scene on that Easter morning when the women arrived at the empty tomb and encountered two angels at the head and foot of the place our Lord was laid to rest. Like the mercy seat, those two angels were testifying that the empty tomb was now the mercy seat where we meet God.

Next, we come to the *table of showbread* found in verses 23–30. This item of furniture was also made of shittim wood overlaid with gold. On this table, God told Moses "to set the show bread before me always" (Exodus 25:30). In this, we again see Jesus. Our hero told us, "Lo, I am with you always" (Matthew 28:20). On the night he was betrayed he spoke, "Take this bread and eat, this is my body...do this in remembrance of me." The *table of showbread* speaks of communion, it speaks of Jesus, the bread which came down from heaven (John 6:41).

After giving Moses the pattern for the table of showbread, God next spoke of the *golden candlestick*, the item we know today as the menorah.

> And thou shalt make a candlestick of pure gold: Of beaten work shall the candlestick be made: His shaft and his branches...six branches shall come out of the side of it [the shaft]; three branches of the candlestick out of the one side, and three branches of the candlestick out of the other side. Three bowls [connectors] made like unto almonds... and in the candlestick [shaft] shall be four bowls made like unto almonds.
>
> Exodus 25:31–34

The candlestick was to be made of pure, yet beaten gold. The gold was not to be heated and molded. God said that this item needed to be beaten into its shape. In this, we see the redeemer's perfect yet brutal sacrifice for us, don't we?

The shaft of the candlestick typifies Jesus, while in the branches, we see those of us who are connected to him. Once again I think of John 15 when Jesus revealed that he is the vine, and we are the branches. And like the candlestick, we too can shine brightly as we stay close to the light.

Lastly, in considering the bowls of almonds, I think of our Lord's resurrection. Almonds were the first fruit harvested in Israel early in the year. Likewise, Paul told us that Jesus was the first fruits of the resurrection (1 Corinthians 15:23). Jesus is seen as the beaten golden candlestick with the connectors of almonds.

After showing Moses the details of the ark, the table, and the candlestick, it came time to tell him of the tabernacle itself. Once again, using our spiritual eyes, we will see Jesus.

> Moreover thou shalt make the tabernacle with ten curtains of fine twined linen [white linen], and blue, and purple, and scarlet: With cherubims and cunning work shalt thou make them.
>
> Exodus 26:1

The inside walls where colorful and beautifully presented. There were angels on the tapestry with a mixture of wonderful blush. But to see this beauty, one had to enter in. Likewise to see Jesus, to see his loveliness and beauty, I too must seek to enter into his presence.

There were ten curtains making up the inner sanctuary. Ten of course, speaks of the law, of the Ten Commandments. It speaks of God's word. Again, Jesus is the word made flesh. Jesus fulfilled the law perfectly. He explained during the Sermon on the Mount discourse that he came not to destroy the law and the prophets but to fulfill (Matthew 5:17). On that dark yet awesome day, when the Savior gave his life for you and me, he said, speaking of the law's fulfillment, "It is finished" (John 19:30).

The four colors of the curtains are seen time and time again in the Bible in pictures of Jesus. Linen (white) pictures the Lord's righteous humanity, blue is the color of heaven and speaks of his abode, purple always typifies his royalty, and of course, the scarlet testifies of his sacrifice.

> And thou shalt make curtains of goats hair to be a covering upon the tabernacle: Eleven curtains shalt thou make.
>
> Exodus 26:7

The middle sheet of the tabernacle was covered with goat's hair! Black would have been the color of that layer. In this level of the tent, we see Jesus dealing with mankind's sins and iniquities. The number eleven also speaks forth a truth. Eleven is a number associated with disorder and of the flesh in the Bible. Certainly, our sins of the flesh have marred our standing with our orderly and perfect maker.

> And thou shalt make a covering for the tent of rams' skin dyed red, and a covering above of badgers' skins.
>
> Exodus 26:14

The last two coverings speak of our Lord's blood shed and of his commonness in becoming one of us. We learn from the key verse in the book of Leviticus that it is the blood that maketh atonement for the soul (Leviticus 17:11). The ram's skins dyed red speak of the blood of the lamb. And badger's skin, the outer covering appeared dull and base in appearance. Nothing beautiful or to be desired would be found in looking at the outside of the tabernacle. No hint of the beauty inside would be suggested in viewing this outer surface. Of course, we remember Isaiah's famous prophecy in describing the Servant to come when thinking of the appearance of the badger's skin. "He hath no form nor comeliness; and when we shall see him, there is no beauty that we should desire him" (Isaiah 53:2). When Jesus came to our planet two thousand years ago, he did not stand out. He appeared as any man, nothing special, nothing to be desired, yet like the inside of the tabernacle, when we look deeper, we see a beauty that is incomparable and incomprehensible!

> And thou shalt make a veil of blue, and purple, and scarlet, and fine twined linen of cunning work: With cherubims shall it be made: And thou shalt hang it upon four pillars of shittim wood overlaid with gold: Their hooks shall be of

> gold, upon four sockets of silver…And the veil shall divide
> unto you between the holy place and the most holy.
>
> Exodus 26:31–33

The tabernacle was to have three distinct sections—the court-yard, the holy place, and the holy of holies. Here, we see that the veil was to divide the holy place from the holy of holies. The holy of holies pictures the place of God's presence, and it was to be partitioned off. We learn from other scriptures that sinful man could not enter into this special place, the place of the holy God. That is without Jesus, for Jesus is again pictured as this veil. He said to the Jews that he was the door to the sheep. "I am the door: By me if any man enter in, he shall be saved" (John 10:9). He later explained to his disciples that he is the way, "I am the way, the truth, and the life: No man cometh to the Father, but by me" (John 14:6). And we see that the veil was to be hung upon four pillars of acacia wood overlaid with gold and that the hooks of gold and four sockets of silver were to support the veil. These four pillars, hooks, and sockets speak of the four gospels. The way to the Father, the door to open to enter in is supported by the gospels, the good news, which tells of our Savior!

> And thou shalt make a hanging for the door of the tent, of
> blue, and purple, and scarlet, and fine twined linen wrought
> with needlework…and for the gate of the court shall be a
> hanging of twenty cubits, of blue, and purple, and scarlet,
> and fine twined linen, wrought with needlework.
>
> Exodus 26:36, 27:16

Here we see that the other two sections of the tabernacle also had the Jesus door. And of course, that is how it must be. We enter in to all aspects of spiritual life via Jesus, for he is the vine, and we are the branches, apart from him we can do nothing (John 15:5).

The outer courtyard pictures our salvation. It was the largest section of the Tabernacle complex and prominently in the courtyard was the altar of sacrifice. Of course, because Jesus became the sacrifice, we can enter into his gates with thanksgiving and into his courts with praise as we too enter into salvation via the veil of the courtyard (John 3:16).

The holy place was to be only entered into by the priests. Once again, the veil must be passed for the priests to enter in. The holy place pictures service to our God. In it were the golden candlestick, the table of showbread, and the altar of incense. These furniture items speak of ministry to people (the candlestick) as we commune with the Father (table of showbread) and in the work and service of prayer (altar of incense).

Lastly, the holy of holies typifies that very special place of God's presence and glory. As the holy place is the place of service to God, the holy of holies is the place of worship to God. The ark of the covenant covered by the mercy seat was the only item of furniture found in the holy of holies. Only the high priest could enter into the holy of holies, and that was but one day per year— the Day of Atonement. Jesus of course, is the great high priest. He entered into the holy of holies, so to speak, on that Passover when he became the sacrifice. On that day, the Bible tells us that the veil, which separated the holy place from the holy of holies in the temple, was torn from top to bottom! Because of the Savior's sacrifice, the way into the holy of holies was now open! No longer was it closed to you and me, but as a holy priesthood, we too can come to the Father as we come boldly before the throne of grace obtaining mercy and finding grace to help in time of need (Hebrews 4:16).

Now before we leave the tabernacle, I must speak of the cross. For just as the way into each of the sections of the tabernacle was bridged by the veil, so too the way into each area of Christian life (pictured by the three tabernacle sections) is bridged by the cross. The outer courtyard picturing salvation points to and stems from the cross. "For God so loved the world, that he gave his only begotten Son, that whosoever believeth in him should not perish, but have everlasting life" (John 3:16).

In the holy place, speaking of that place of Christian service and works, we see the cross. "Whosoever will come after me, let him deny himself, and take up his cross, and follow me" (Mark 8:34). And lastly, in the holy place, that place of worship before the Lord we again see the cross. "And he took bread, and gave thanks, and brake it, and gave unto them, saying, This is my body which is given for you: This do in remembrance of me" (Luke 22:19).

The Bible ends this section of the tabernacle and its furniture by speaking of the altar of sacrifice. Here again, we understand that the altar points to the cross—that holy place where Jesus became the sacrifice and was figuratively burnt as a sweet-smelling sacrifice for you and me. This item was actually in the courtyard outside of the tabernacle and was the first thing that a person would see upon passing the veil into the tabernacle complex.

> And thou shalt make an altar of shittim wood...and thou shalt overlay it with brass...all the vessels thereof thou shalt make of brass. And thou shalt make for it a grate of network of brass; and upon the net shalt thou make four brazen rings in the four corners thereof...and thou shalt make staves for the altar, staves of shittim wood, and overlay them with brass.
>
> Exodus 27:1–6 (excerpts)

The altar was the place where the sacrifices would be burnt as a sweet savor unto the Lord. It was outside of the tabernacle just as Jesus was taken outside of the camp. In being overlaid with brass, we see another truth—for brass is the metal which speaks of judgment in the Bible. We will consider this type again when we look at the brazen serpent, which Moses lifted up in the wilderness in a few chapters hence.

Yes, Jesus became sin for us, our sins were judged in him so that we could be made righteous in God's sight, so that we could have the righteousness of God in him (2 Corinthians 5:21). Praise him for his wonderful sacrifice!

For further study:

1. In 1 Samuel 6 when the men of Bethshemesh removed the mercy seat to make sure the law was still in the Ark of the Covenant, what happened to them? Why is this a picture of what happens to people when they promote judgment over mercy?

2. The four colors of the curtains, white, blue, purple & red speaking of our Lord's humanity, heavenliness, royalty & sacrifice also speak of the four gospels. Which gospel do you suppose correlates with the color purple? Which one highlights the red of his sacrifice? How about the white of his humanness? Which one is blue?

3. Gold is associated with Christ's glory & diety, acacia wood with his humanness & brass with judgment. Can you look for examples of silver in the Bible? What does silver represent?

The Sabbath, the Seventh-Year Sabbatical, and the Jubilee: Pictures of our Rest in Christ

The Weekly Sabbath

AFTER GOD CREATED the heavens and the earth, the Bible states that he rested on the seventh day (Genesis 2:2).

> And God blessed the seventh day, and sanctified it: Because that in it he had rested from all his work which he had made.
>
> Genesis 2:3

166 DANIEL TOMLINSON, M.D.

Now fast forward to the days of Moses. In giving his children the law, God said to his children to take a day off every week to honor the seventh day, the Sabbath. This was radical news to the children of Israel. At that time, no other ethnic groups were resting from their labor. Life was meant to be hard, and work had to be done.

But God didn't just say take a day off if you want. He said, if you don't rest, if you don't give worth to the Sabbath, you will die.

> Ye shall keep the Sabbath therefore; for it is holy unto you: Every one that defileth it shall surely be put to death: For whosoever doeth any work therein, that soul shall be cut off from among his people.
>
> Exodus 31:14

You see, God was painting a picture here. He was and is saying that it's not about the work we do, it's not about the effort we put forth, but it's about what he has already done! In the Sabbath, we see a picture of Christ and the work that he has accomplished on our behalf. That is, because Jesus did the work, because he paid the price, we get to rest. In other words, the Sabbath is an Old Testament type of the New Testament principle, which states that it is by grace through faith and not of works that you are saved (Ephesians 2:8–9). The Sabbath pictures that rest we have in Jesus. We can't earn our salvation, and by resting, we give worth to the finished work to that completed sacrifice of the Son!

Now I see why not honoring the Sabbath resulted in death. In this portrait, God is painting, working on the Sabbath is akin to working for my salvation. That too results in death. It's by faith alone that we are saved. Not our works. If I feel I must add to Christ's finished work, then I too will die. Oh, not literally, but I will miss out on the blessing he has for me as I rest in him.

So our rest in Christ, our Sabbath really comes down to faith. Am I going to believe what God tells me, or am I going to keep trying to work things out on my own? Paul asked that same question to the Colossians when he exhorted,

> As ye have therefore received Christ Jesus the Lord [by faith], so walk ye in him:
>
> Colossians 2:6

It's by faith you are saved, but now go out and work to please God. That's the trap they fell into. No, no, no, we can't do anything in our flesh to please God. Only by faith can we please him (Hebrews 11:6). Our good works are only the response to the grace and mercy we have received from Him. Not any kind of payback for the gift he has given. If the gift of salvation required me to work after receiving it, it wouldn't be a gift! Thus, as I have received Jesus, i.e. by faith, so I must walk in him, again, walk by faith!

So we come back to the Sabbath, to our rest, to Christ.

> There remaineth therefore a rest [Sabbath] to the people of God. For he that is entered into his rest, he also hath ceased from his own works, as God did from his.
>
> Hebrews 4:9–10

The person who rests in the finished work of Christ, who stops laboring for salvation but just believes God, that person has ceased from working just as God rested from his work of creation on the seventh day.

A wonderful perk of resting in the finished work, of resting in Jesus, is found a few verses later.

> Let us therefore come boldly unto the throne of grace, that we may obtain mercy, and find grace to help in time of need.
>
> Hebrews 4:16

Because of the finished work of Christ, we can come boldly before the Father before the God of the universe and receive help in time of need. How cool is that!

THE SEVENTH-YEAR SABBATICAL

The law of Moses prescribed a second point of rest for the children of Israel called the year of release. Every seventh year, God's kids were to take a break. It was to be a time when farming ceased, giving the land rest from overproduction (Exodus 23:10–11). Two other unusual occurrences were to be in play. That is, every seventh year all debts were to be forgiven, and all servants were to be set free (Deuteronomy 15:1–2, 15). Of course, these three requirements of the year of release go completely against our human nature. We feel we need to keep working not realizing that it truly is God who is our sufficiency. And we certainly don't relish forgiving a loan or sending away an employee with a golden parachute.

But when you think about this from the point of view of the land, the debtor, and the servant, then we learn something beautiful. You see, we are not the farmer, the creditor, or the master; God is! We are the overworked land, the destitute debtor, and the hopeless servant. We are the ones needing release, not the ones giving it. The year of release is what Jesus did for us. He gives us rest from our labors. Our debt is cancelled, and wonderfully, we are set free. We are no longer servants to the law of sin and death!

Truly, yet another Old Testament picture of Jesus is seen in the Seventh-Year Sabbatical.

THE JUBILEE

Every fifty years, a special year called the Jubilee was to occur in Israel. Like the year of release, all debts were to be cancelled, and all servants were to be set free, but in addition, a new act of mercy was prescribed.

> And ye shall hallow the fiftieth year, and proclaim liberty throughout all the land unto all the inhabitants thereof: It

shall be a jubilee unto you; and ye shall return every man unto his possession, and ye shall return every man unto his family.

Leviticus 25:10

In addition to release, the fiftieth year provided restoration. Not only were debts cancelled and servants set free, but in the Year of Jubilee, the people were given back the property they had lost over the proceeding forty-nine years due to their bad investing habits and poor lifestyle choices. In this, we again see what our Lord has and will do for us, for we too have lost much in our journey through this life—lost relationships, lost opportunities, and lost peace due to our rebelliousness and disobedience. But God wants to restore what we have lost. In fact, he promises to do that in the age to come. Look with me at the words of Joel in speaking of the millennial time frame.

And I will restore to you the years that the locust hath eaten, the cankerworm, and the caterpillar, and the palmerworm, my great army which I sent among you. And you shall eat in plenty, and be satisfied, and praise the name of the Lord your God, that hath dealt wondrously with you: And my people shall never be ashamed. And ye shall know that I am in the midst of Israel, and that I am the Lord thy God.

Joel 2:25–27

Those things we have lost will be restored. Relationships gone sour, opportunities squandered, peace departed. How will he restore these things? I'm not sure, but he promises it, and the Jubilee Year pictures it, so I choose to believe it! Hope you will too!

For further study:

1. When the children of Israel gathered manna on the Sabbath, what happened to it? Why is working on the Sabbath a picture of not trusting God?

2. Since we are the overworked land, the destitute debtor and the hopeless servant given release by God, how does that help you relate to the problems & circumstances of others? Does it make you want to help people more?

3. Is God a capitalist? How does the Fifty Year Jubilee set safety parameters upon capitalism?

THE RED HEIFER: THE
PURIFICATION FOR SIN

O N THE ROAD to Emmaus, Jesus certainly must have mentioned the typology associated with the Israel's red heifer. The similarities of this sacrifice scream out crying, "this is Jesus, look, this is what we did to him!"

> This is the ordinance of the law which the Lord hath commanded, saying, Speak to the children of Israel, that they bring thee a red heifer without spot, wherein is no blemish, and upon which never came yoke.
>
> Numbers 19:2

A red heifer was rare. An uncommon recessive gene is what scientifically allowed a cow to be completely red. Likewise, Jesus, as the only begotten of the Father, is unique. He is one of a kind just as the red heifer would be at any given time in Israel. Also the sacrifice was to be without spot and blemish. In Jesus, we see his beauty, perfection, and sinlessness illustrated, don't we? Lastly, no yoke was to have come upon that animal. Jesus, of course, in his walk was never under any human control or authority.

> And ye shall bring her unto…the priest (the high priest), that he may bring her forth without the camp, and one (another) shall slay her before his face.
>
> Numbers 19:3

This verse makes me cry as I consider that the Jews do not see this! This is exactly what happened to the rabbi called Yeshua! On the night of his passion, the cohort of men brought Jesus to the high priest, Caiaphas. He arranged for Jesus to be taken outside of the camp (Calvary) where another (the Romans) slew Jesus before his (Caiaphas's) face!

Of note, this was the only sacrifice that the priests did not actually slay themselves. All others—the bulls, goats, lambs, and birds were sacrificed directly by the priests to reveal to the people the seriousness of their sins. Once again, the uniqueness of this sacrifice points to our Lord's matchless offering!

> And…the (high) priest shall take of her blood with his finger, and sprinkle of her blood directly before the tabernacle of the congregation seven times.
>
> Numbers 19:4

Seven is that perfect number speaking of completeness. In this case, the blood of the heifer completely purifies just as does the blood of the redeemer. We also remember that our Savior was pierced in seven places to which I think this verse also speaks. His hands, feet, back, head, and side were all bloodied to cleanse us from our sin.

> And one shall burn the heifer in his sight; her skin, and her flesh, and her blood, with her dung, shall he burn.
>
> Numbers 19:5

This sacrifice was completely consumed by fire. It was dramatic. It was disturbing. It was fierce. In like manner, the consuming fire of the Father's wrath toward sin came down upon the one of whom the red heifer speaks.

> And the priest shall take cedar wood, and hyssop, and scarlet, and cast it into the midst of the burning of the heifer.
>
> Numbers 19:6

These three items come up time and time again as pictures found portraying the crucifixion story—the cedar wood of his cross, the hyssop wood likely used to deliver his blows when he was scourged, and the scarlet blood that he shed.

> Then the priest shall wash his clothes, and he shall bathe his flesh in water…and the priest shall be unclean.
>
> Numbers 19:7

This offering is particularly singled out as defiling the high priest. Likewise, Caiaphas and the Jews also despoiled themselves in condemning the one pictured in this sacrifice. And in their refusal to cleanse thereafter, they permanently cursed themselves.

> And a man that is clean shall gather up the ashes of the heifer, and lay them up without the camp in a clean place.
>
> Numbers 19:9a

This of course prophesizes of how Joseph of Arimathea, a clean man not involved in the brutal activities of that day, gathered up our Lord's fleshly carcass and placed him in a new tomb wherein no man had been laid.

> And it shall be kept for the congregation of the children of Israel. It is a purification for sin.
>
> Numbers 19:9b

For the children of Israel, this is the purpose of the sacrifice of the red heifer. It was the purification for sin. It was the payment for sin. Likewise, in considering the meaning of the word *Israel* for those who are governed by God, those believers who have submitted to God, our Lord's sacrifice is the purification for sin!

What a picture indeed! As I said, the sacrifice of the red heifer can only be sounding one call, one song, and one name—Jesus!

Now before we leave this sacrifice, there's one more interesting and unusual detail to consider. That is, this offering was particularly singled out to be female. No other sacrifice was required to be of Eve's gender. It didn't matter for goats, lambs, and birds. Of course the sacrifice of bulls by definition needs to be male. But here, we have the only female sacrifice. How does that relate to Jesus? The answer lies in one of the names of God. He is God Almighty. In Hebrew, that is El Shaddai.

You see, Jesus is complete. He is the one who upholds everything by the word of his power (Hebrews 1:3), yet he also is the One who seeks out the one lost sheep, tells the children to come to him, and like a mother tells us, he will never leave or forsake us. Unlike Adam who needed to marry Eve to be completed (Genesis 2:24), Jesus is whole in himself. He is both masculine and feminine. He is the sacrificed bull, and he is the red heifer. He is the one and only El Shaddai!

For further study:

1. The ashes of the red heifer were collected and used in various purification ceremonies. What New Testament activity does this portray?

2. The defiled high priest was to bathe his flesh in water. Now a fountain or a river of running water pictures the Spirit. What does bath water picture in the Bible? Hint... see Psalm 119:9

THE BRAZEN SERPENT:
IF I BE LIFTED UP

D ID YOU KNOW that murmuring and complaining should be added to the list of the seven deadly sins? Time and time again in the book of Numbers, we see the children of Israel murmuring against Moses and ultimately against God. Every time it led to calamity as will be the result in the story we are about to consider. But as often is the case, God, the gracious one, will find a way to forgive his children just like he does for you and me when we murmur and complain.

The story really starts in chapter twenty of Numbers. There, we see that Israel was denied permission by their brother Edom to pass through his border on their way to Canaan. Instead of asking God whether they should proceed forth and take on Edom if necessary, they diverted west into the brutal Negev desert. Thus, they became discouraged, which led to their murmuring.

> And they journeyed from mount Hor by the way of the
> Red sea, to compass the land of Edom: And the soul of the
> people was much discouraged because of the way.
>
> Numbers 21:4

As an aside, Edom, the children of Esau, always picture the
flesh in the Old Testament. Esau was Jacob's twin brother who
sold his birthright for a pot of stew. He was not sensitive to the
God of his father, Isaac, just as the flesh is not sensitive to the
things of the Spirit. When Rebekah, Jacob, and Esau's mother was
pregnant with the twins, God told her that her two boys would
be two types of people who would always be at odds against each
other, perfectly picturing the battle between the flesh and the
spirit that these two portray.

So we see that in diverting around Edom, the children of
Israel are picturing how giving into the flesh will lead to trouble.
We are told to send the flesh away, to crucify the flesh, not to put
up with it as clearly Israel did in our story before us. Thus, they
became discouraged and began to murmur.

> And the people spake against God, and against Moses,
> Wherefore have ye brought us up out of Egypt to die in
> the wilderness? For there is no bread, neither is there any
> water; and our soul loathe this light bread.
>
> Numbers 21:5

Do you remember that water in scripture portrays God's Spirit?
The people were in a dry place, which can of course be spiritual-
ized for us. When I get dry spiritually, I too will often murmur.

And look, they "loathed this light bread!" They were sick of
the manna that God was daily providing. This is serious! For we
remember that Jesus said of himself that he is the true bread come
down from heaven. Manna pictures the Lord as we discussed earlier. In loathing "this light bread" the people were pushing away
their source of nourishment and provision. Unfortunately, we all

too often do that too, don't we? "I can do this myself" we say, forgetting that Jesus, the manna from heaven, is the true vine that provides all of our needs. And without him, without Jesus, the word of God says we can do nothing (John 15:5)!

So the people murmured and complained. Next, we see the repercussions of this deadly sin, which we so often trivialize.

> And the Lord sent fiery serpents among the people, and they bit the people: And much people of Israel died.
>
> Numbers 21:6

In the Old Testament, when it says that the Lord sent or caused some calamity, we need to remember that it means he allows it, that he removes his protection. "For the wages of sin is death" (Romans 6:23), "your sins have hid his face from you" (Isaiah 59:2). God is good, He doesn't slam us when we sin, but our sin itself brings death and destruction!

Thus, we see in the case of murmuring and complaining that serpents (clearly a picture of Satan and his minions) are given free reign to bite and kill those caught up in this sin. So realizing their error, the people did a smart thing. They called upon the Lord for deliverance. The thing I need to remember to do also!

> Therefore the people came to Moses, and said, we have sinned, for we have spoken against the Lord, and against thee: Pray unto the Lord, that he may take away the serpents from us. And Moses prayed for the people. And the Lord said unto Moses, Make thee a fiery (brass) serpent, and set it upon a pole: And it shall come to pass, that every one that is bitten, when he shall look upon it, shall live. And Moses made a serpent of brass, and put it upon a pole, and it came to pass, that if a serpent had bitten any man, when he beheld the serpent of brass, he lived.
>
> Numbers 21:7–9

This typology shouts of Jesus' sacrifice! Because of our sin and depravity, because of our murmuring and complaining, the serpent (Satan) has been free to bite and ultimately to kill us. But we too, can look to Jesus—the one who became sin for us, the one who became the brass serpent who was lifted up on the cross of Calvary, and just as the men of Israel who looked upon the brazen serpent, we too will live!

Yes, truly Jesus became the brazen serpent.

> For he hath made him to be sin for us, who knew no sin:
> That we might be made the righteousness of God in him.
>
> 2 Corinthians 5:21

Jesus pointed out this Old Testament story as a figure of him on that famous night the priest Nicodemus learned that to be saved, he must be born again.

> And as Moses lifted up the serpent in the wilderness, even so must the Son of man be lifted up: That whosoever believeth in him shall not perish, but have eternal life. For God so loved the world, that he gave his only begotten Son, that whosoever believeth in him shall not perish, but have everlasting life.
>
> John 3:14–16

No doubt, on the road to Emmaus, our Savior certainly spoke of the brazen serpent, which was lifted up so that all who would embrace his sacrifice would live.

Thank you, Lord, for taking my sin!

For further study:

1. We are told to crucify the flesh. How does one do that? For help on this question, see Romans 6.

2. If a man of Israel refused to follow Moses' instructions to look upon the brazen serpent, what happened to that man? What New Testament principle does this portray?

3. The brass serpent is the coat of arms for the American Medical Association. Why do you imagine they chose that symbol for their group?

THE LAW OF VOWS: COVERED BY OUR HUSBAND

And Moses spake unto the heads of the tribes concerning the children of Israel, saying, This is the thing which the Lord hath commanded. If a man vow a vow unto the Lord, or swear an oath to bind his soul with a bond; he shall not break his word, he shall do according to all that proceedeth out of his mouth.

Numbers 30:1–2

HERE WE LEARN of God's view of vows and of promises made. The covenant maker states that if I make a vow to the Lord, then I should keep it! If I say to the Lord, "Dear God, if you prosper my endeavor, I will give back to you 50 percent of the profits," then God expects me to keep that promise, no matter how outrageous or ill advised that oath may be! In reflecting upon this law, I find much comfort. That's because God, the promise keeper, will not hold man to a higher standard than what he himself would keep! If God makes a promise to me, then I know he will keep it. "I will never leave you or forsake you" is a done deal! "In my Father's house are many mansions. I go to prepare a place for you" is going to happen! "There is no condemnation to those who are in Christ Jesus"(Romans 8:1). Not guilty, this cries!

> If a woman also vow a vow unto the Lord, and bind herself by a bond…and if she had at all an husband when she vowed, or uttered ought out of her lips, wherewith she bound her soul; and her husband heard it, and held his peace at her in the day that he heard it: Then her vow shall stand, and her bonds wherewith she bound her soul shall stand. But if her husband disallowed her on the day that he heard it; then he shall make the vow which she vowed, and that which she uttered with her lips, wherewith she bound her soul, of none effect: And the Lord shall forgive her.
>
> Numbers 30:3, 6–8

Oh, oh, here we go again with the Bible and its antiquated and chauvinistic ways! The man has to keep his vows, but the woman doesn't. I don't know if I like that you may say. Well, consider the spiritual level of this law, and I think you may see it differently. You see, we are all women; we are the bride of Christ. Throughout the Bible, many times when women are spoken of an application to our relationship with our husband can be easily seen. This is the case here! Jesus, of course, is the husband in this picture. He is the promise keeper, who always will keep his vows. Unfortunately, we don't always keep ours! I may promise God something in sincerity, only later to find I am unable or unwilling to carry it through! Well, thank God for the law of vows. As the woman in the relationship, my husband immediately knows when I make a vow I can't keep, and He will lovingly disallow it!

Jesus will say to the Father, "You know, Abba, Dan means well when he says he's going to wake up every morning and pray for the peace of Jerusalem, but he can't really keep that oath. As his husband, I'm going to void that one!" And just like that, I am forgiven and cleansed from the promise I made but could not keep.

We see this play out wonderfully in Peter's story. When Jesus told his disciples that on the night of his betrayal, all would forsake him, Peter immediately promised that even if all forsook the Lord, that he would not! Of course Jesus disallowed that oath, didn't he! The lamb of God told his disciple, no, that's not going to happen, Peter, for before the cock crow this night, not only will you leave me, but you will indeed deny me. But good news, I have prayed for you, and when you are recovered I have a job for you, I want you to strengthen the others! (Luke 22:31-34) Jesus voided Peter's promise and lovingly cleared him of the shame he would feel when his lack of commitment came to pass. This is what he does for you and me too!

> But every vow of a widow, and of her that is divorced, wherewith they have bound their souls, shall stand against her.
>
> Numbers 30:9

An unmarried woman is held to the same standard as a man. So those who still feel that the woman is sort of being treated as second class in this story can just remain unmarried! Of course, in the typology and flow of this law, being unmarried is a picture of being unsaved of not having a relationship with the redeemer, Jesus Christ. Without the covering of our husband, then we are not forgiven when we make promises to God we cannot keep. As the unbeliever promises in his heart to be a good person expecting that to earn his way into heaven, well, that promise just isn't going to happen, and unfortunately for that unmarried soul, it is not forgiven, and it is not covered!

Thus, on that wonderful road to Emmaus, Jesus may have pointed out the law of the vows, and how he as our husband is seen wonderfully as the covering for our many foolish and silly promises, which we make but cannot keep.

For further study:

1. Have you ever promised something to God only to renege on that promise? Does the law of vows bless you?

2. An unmarried woman pictures the unbelieving person. Who does a widow typify in the flow of this story? Can a person loose their salvation? Can a person walk away from their salvation?

3. Do you find 1 Timothy 2:9-15 easier to understand if you spiritually see women in this section as all people, men or women, who are married to Christ?

THE CITY OF REFUGE: COVERED BY THE LIFE OF THE HIGH PRIEST

As YOU MAY remember, the literal promised land, which the children of Israel were to take in the Old Testament, is a picture, is a type of the Spirit-filled life for us in New Testament times. Just like God called Israel to take the territory, he calls you and me to move into the land of victory and rest, which comes by walking with him in the spirit! But in the land, there were still battles. There were still problems for the Jews just like we can still encounter difficulty and troubles in our lives in this day. Such is the case when we consider the cities of refuge.

> And the Lord spake unto Moses saying, Speak unto the children of Israel, and say unto them, When ye be come over Jordan into the land of Canaan; Then ye shall appoint

> you cities to be cities of refuge for you; that the slayer may flee thither, which killeth any person unawares. And they shall be unto you cities for refuge from the avenger; that the manslayer die not, until he stand before the congregation in judgment.

> Numbers 35:9–12

God made a provision for his children for forgiveness when a person committed second-degree murder. That is, when a man killed another person out of passion, not out of malice and premeditation, he could get relief from his crime by rushing to the city of refuge. The avenger had the right to kill the manslayer in that time unless the slayer sought sanctuary in the city of refuge. Then the avenger had no right to kill the man caught up in second-degree murder, but it was up to the congregation to decide the slayer's fate.

> But if he thrust him of hatred, or hurl at him by laying of wait, that he die; or of in enmity smite him with his hand, that he die: He that smote him shall surely be put to death; for he is a murderer: The revenger of blood shall slay the murderer, when he meeteth him.

> Numbers 35:20–21

Premeditated killing, first-degree murder, was not covered though. The city of refuge was not going to save in that circumstance.

Now, if the congregation decided that second-degree murder had occurred, then the following regulations were in play:

> And the congregation shall deliver the slayer out of the hand of the revenger of blood, and the congregation shall restore him to the city of his refuge, whither he was fled: And he shall abide in it unto the death of the high priest, which was anointed with holy oil. But if the slayer shall at any time come without the border of the city of his refuge, whither he was fled; and the revenger of blood find him without the borders of the city of his refuge, and the

revenger of blood kill the slayer; he shall not be guilty of blood: Because he should have remained in the city of his refuge until the death of the high priest: But after the death of the high priest the slayer shall return into the land of his possession [he was free after the death of the high priest].

Numbers 35:24–28

So here we see that if the verdict of the congregation was indeed second degree and not first -degree murder, then the manslayer could stay safely in the city of refuge. He would be covered and protected in the city. He was still guilty, but the punishment was stayed. But if the slayer left the protection of the city of refuge, then the avenger had every right to kill the manslayer. Significantly though, after the death of the high priest, then the manslayer was free to return to his possession. At that time, the avenger no longer had any right over the slayer to kill him, no matter where the slayer resided. At that time, the manslayer was pronounced not guilty!

In this we see Jesus, don't we? Christ of course is the city of refuge. He is the name that we flee to be saved from our sins. But he is also the high priest. His life covers our guilt and shame while we live safely in the city of refuge just as the manslayer was safe as he stayed ensconced in the city of refuge. The avenger of course is the devil. The Bible states that Satan is the accuser of the brethren. He comes before God, noting we are sinners deserving of death. Indeed we are, but the Father sees you and me covered by the life of the high priest. The sentence is stayed. He cannot destroy you and me. But upon the death of the high priest, something wonderful happened. The manslayer was now free. Likewise, the death of our great high priest has freed me from the sentence I had placed over my head. I too am not guilty! Same for you!

Now, two more important points to ponder. We see in this analogy that God makes a distinction between first- and second-degree murder. That is, one type of evil is covered and eventually erased while the other is not protected and not forgiven. This doesn't sound right as the Bible teaches that the blood of the Savior saves us from all sin. How does this type hold up when we consider this apparent discrepancy? Well, the answer lies in the fact that, indeed, all sin can be forgiven but not all sinners will be forgiven. You see, the manslayer that commits second-degree murder is analogous to those of us who struggle with sin, who feel guilty by our sin, who are bothered when we sin. In contrast, the man who kills out of hatred and premeditation pictures the one who is not convicted by his sin, who is not sorry for his sin, who feels no remorse when he sins. He is the one who practices sin, the one who only gets better at sinning. The Bible tells of this man with these serious words.

> Now the works of the flesh are manifest, which are these; Adultery, fornication, uncleanness, lasciviousness, idolatry, witchcraft, hatred, variance, emulations, wrath, strife, seditions, heresies, envyings, murders, drunkenness, revellings, and such like: Of the which I tell you before, as I have also told you in time past, that they which do such things shall not inherit the kingdom of God.
>
> Galatians 5:19–21

A better rendering of the last verse should be, "They that practice such things" instead of the weaker English translation of "they that do such things shall not inherit the kingdom." These words are not for the man or woman who is accidentally caught up in these sins. That person who is guilt-ridden by his adultery, his wrath, his drunkenness, and the other sins listed is pictured by the manslayer that killed without hatred and premeditation. But the person who committed first-degree murder is the one seen here as practicing evil, the one not bothered by his sin, the one that the city of refuge cannot save.

The second point is seen when the manslayer left the city of refuge prior to the death of the high priest. At that point, the avenger of blood had the right to kill him. This of course pictures the man or woman who walks away from their salvation. Indeed, I cannot lose my salvation; I am eternally secure. But I could walk away from it! I could say that Jesus is no longer for me. I could turn my back on him. I could reject his gift of salvation. I could leave the city of refuge!

The Bible pictures this truth over and over in its pages. If Noah would have left the ark, he would have be destroyed. Paul told the shipmates on that stormy night on the Mediterranean Sea that unless they stayed in the ship, they could not be saved. If Rahab and her family would have left their home, which had the red thread hanging out of the window, they would have been slain when Jericho was taken. And if the children of Israel had not covered their doorposts with the blood of a lamb, the angel of death would have not passed over their abodes. Truly, when Judas betrayed his Lord, the words spoken were, "It would be better if that man had never been born." This is an important point. I am saved by the blood. It is not just a one-time thing; it really means that I am continually saved by the blood. And I'm glad for that as I've still been sinning since that day in 1973 when I first realized what the redeemer had done for me in forgiving my sins. I'm glad I'm continually saved, and I'm not going to leave the city of refuge!

For further study:

1. The manslayer would flee to the city of refuge and the congregation would then decide if he had committed first or second-degree murder. What New Testament precept does this typify?

2. The city of refuge protected a manslayer if he killed a person unawares. Have you ever killed a person unawares? Have you caused another to stumble in their faith because of your words or actions?

3. The Promised Land is pictured as the spirit-filled life in Bible typology. After the death of the high priest the slayer was free to return to his possession. What spiritual principle does this reveal?

THE BOND SERVANT:
THE PIERCED SLAVE

IN THE ANCIENT world, when a man or a family became destitute, they would sell themselves as servants, slaves really, in order to obtain protection, food, and raiment. Working for the company store was the lot for many souls of antiquity as often slavery made economic sense. So it was in the nation of Israel. The poor of the land would attach themselves to the wealthy in order to subsist. This type of bondage was, and is not God's heart for his people. Thus, as we have discussed earlier, God put parameters over the children of Israel so the rich could not take advantage of their economic position in a cruel way.

> For the poor shall never cease out of the land: Therefore I command thee, saying, Thou shalt open thine hand wide unto thy brother, to thy poor, and to the needy in the land. And if thy brother, an Hebrew man, or an Hebrew woman,

be sold unto thee, and serve thee six years; then in the seventh year thou shalt let him go free from thee. And when thou sendest him out free from thee, thou shalt not let him go away empty: Thou shalt furnish him liberally out of thy flock, and out of thy floor, and out of thy winepress: Of that wherewith the Lord thy God hath blessed thee thou shalt give unto him. And thou shalt remember that thou wast a bondman in the land of Egypt, and the Lord thy God redeemed thee: Therefore I command thee this thing today.

Deuteronomy 15:11–15

God commanded the wealthy man that his poor brother and his family were only to be in servanthood for six years and then were to be released. But not only were they to be set free, but the master would build them up financially so as to cause them to succeed without needing to return to bondage. In this way, the poor of the land were given an opportunity to break free from the economic position that life can often throw a person's way!

But occasionally, a man and his family would prefer to stay under the covering of the master. God's provision for that is seen in the next verses.

And it shall be, if he say unto thee, I will not go away from thee; because he lovest thee and thine house, because he is well with thee; Then thou shalt take an aul, and thrust it though his ear unto the door, and he shall be thy servant forever. And also thy maidservant thou shalt do likewise.

Deuteronomy 15:16–17

The man or the woman who would desire to stay with the master would have his or her ear pierced! That servant was now called a bond servant. He would voluntarily offer up his body to be pierced with a nail into the wood of the door.

Of course, in this we see Jesus! He too became poor, becoming a servant and was voluntarily pierced in order to be with us forever!

> Let this mind be in you, which was also in Christ Jesus: Who, being in the form of God, thought it not robbery to be equal with God: But made himself of no reputation, and took upon him the form of a servant, and was made in the likeness of men: And being found in the fashion as a man, he humbled himself, and became obedient unto death, even the death of the cross.
>
> Philippians 2:5–8

Jesus became a slave. He became a bond servant so he could be with us, the real servants, forever. How crazy is that!

But the servant is not greater than the master. Just as he was willing to go to the cross, to be pierced for you and me, so too he told us to do the same.

> Then said Jesus to his disciples, If any man will come after me, let him deny himself, and take up his cross, and follow me.
>
> Matthew 16:24

Just as our Lord became the bond servant, so must we. I should be willing to sacrificially die to self in order to see redemption in others. When I do this, the next verse tells me I will find life.

> For whosoever will save his life shall lose it: And whosoever will lose his life for my sake shall find it.
>
> Matthew 16:25

Oh, the great paradoxes of God's word—give and you will receive; the first shall be last and the last shall be first; lose your life, and you will live! Indeed, God's ways are not like our ways!

Jesus modeled our response to his servanthood when he demonstrated how the disciples were to serve one another.

> And supper being ended...He laid aside his garments, and took a towel...and began to wash the disciples feet...So after he had washed their feet...and was set down again, he said to them, Know ye what I have done to you? Ye call me Master and Lord; and ye say well, for so I am. If I then, your Lord and Master have washed your feet; ye also ought to wash one another's feet. For I have given you an example, that you should do as I have done to you...If you know these things, happy are you if ye do them.
>
> John 13:2–17 (excerpts)

Jesus taught that servanthood is a key to happiness. That's right. He said, happy are you, happy I'll be, if we do these things, if we serve one another.

We see the end result of serving others, of letting go of our wants for the good of others, and of dying for others as we look at Jesus.

> Wherefore God also hath highly exalted him, and given him a name which is above every name: That at the name of Jesus every knee should bow...and every tongue should confess that Jesus Christ is Lord, to the glory of God the Father.
>
> Philippians 2:9–11

For further study:

1. The slave was to be freed in the seventh year. How is God's plan for the ages, from Genesis to Revelation, framed in this statement?

2. When the slave was set free he was given gifts so as to not return to bondage. What is pictured in that?

3. The servant who chose to stay with his master had a nail thrust through his ear, the organ of hearing, into and against a wooden door, the entrance to another place. What is being said by God in type with the nail, ear, wood & door?

THE TREE OF LIFE:
BIBLE BOOKENDS

WE ARE INTRODUCED to the tree of life after Adam and Eve sinned in eating of that other famous tree found in Eden known as the tree of the knowledge of good and evil.

> And the Lord God said, behold, the man has become as one of us, to know good and evil: And now, lest he put forth his hand, and take also of the tree of life, and eat, and live forever: Therefore the Lord God sent him forth from the garden of Eden, to till the ground from whence he was taken. So he drove out the man; and he placed at the east of the garden of Eden Cherubims and a flaming sword which turned every way, to keep the way of the tree of life.
>
> Genesis 3:22–24

Adam and Eve were in an innocent state as they dwelt in Eden. They were children, really, with no concept of evil. They did not practice nor even think of evil. God instructed them continually as they relied upon him for fellowship and instruction. But their maker did give them a choice. He told the man that he was not to eat of the tree of the knowledge of good and evil. For in the day he ate of that tree, God told Adam, he would surely die! God gave the man the choice out of love. God does not force our love upon him. Thus, in order to receive Adam's love, God needed to allow that first man the choice between walking with him verses going out on his own. When Adam and Eve ate of that tree, they in essence were saying that they wanted to be in control; they wanted to be the masters of their own destiny; they wanted to be their own gods! That's why the creator needed to drive them from Eden. They were no longer innocent children but had become sophisticated and independent adults! And with the tree of life present in the garden, God could not allow the couple to eat of it and live forever in their sinful and unredeemed state.

Of course, Jesus is that tree of life as he likely explained to those men on the road to Emmaus. He is the vine, and we are the branches. His body was broken for us so that in eating of him, we are made whole.

The tree of life is found again at the end of the book. This time, since Adam's race has been redeemed, the fruit of that tree is available for mankind to partake of.

> And he showed me a pure river of water of life, clear as crystal, proceeding out of the throne of God and of the Lamb. In the midst of the street of it, and on either side of the river, was the tree of life, which bear twelve manner of fruits, and yielded her fruit every month: And the leaves of the tree were for the healing of the nations.
>
> Revelation 22:1–2

Indeed, Jesus is the one who heals all of our diseases. He is called the balm of Gilead. He is Jehovah Raphe (the God who heals). By his stripes, we are healed!

Elsewhere in the Old Testament, we see our Lord likened to a life-giving tree.

> And there shall come forth a rod out of the stem of Jesse, and a Branch shall grow out of his roots: And the spirit of the Lord shall rest upon him, the spirit of wisdom and understanding, the spirit of counsel and might, the spirit of knowledge and of the fear of the Lord.
>
> Isaiah 11:1–2

And after telling the Jewish exiles in Babylon that the kingdom of Judah under the authority of Zedekiah was like a cedar tree that will be cut down, Ezekiel tells of another great tree that will spring up to rule over the other trees in glory and majesty.

> Thus saith the Lord God; I will also take of the highest branch of the high cedar, and will set it; I will crop off the top of his young twigs a tender one, and will plant it upon an high mountain an eminent. In the mountain of the height of Israel will I plant it: And it shall bring forth boughs, and bear fruit, and be a goodly cedar...And all the trees of the field shall know that I the Lord have brought down the high tree [Zedekiah's rule], have exalted the low tree [Jesus the low and meek one], have dried up the green tree and have made the dry tree to flourish: I the Lord have spoken and have done it.
>
> Ezekiel 17:22–24

Yes, the tree of life, which was originally guarded by the cherubim and the flaming sword is seen at the end of the book as an accessible and exalted cedar, which bringeth forth healing fruit for all to enjoy.

What a story, what a hope, what a promise.

For further study:

1. What do you suppose are the twelve manner of fruit which the tree of life will yield from month to month in the age to come?

2. The tree of life is found in the midst of a pure river on that future day. In Bible typology, what is this speaking of?

3. Look at Psalm 34:8. What spiritual associations do you make?

PART 3

PROPHECIES PROCLAIMING JESUS

T HERE ARE MANY, many prophetic writings telling of the savior's physical visitation to our world, far too numerous for me to cover in totality in this little book. Also, in studying the prophetical writings, it is important to remember that God's revelation to the Jews in the Old Testament was a progressive word. Peter tells us clearly that the Old Testament actually speaks of two visitations, which are separated in time and have differing purposes.

> Receiving the end of your faith, even the salvation of your souls. Of which salvation the prophets have enquired and searched diligently, who prophesied of the grace that should come unto you: Searching what, or what manner of time the Spirit which was in them did signify, when it testified beforehand the sufferings of Christ (His First Coming) and the glory that should follow (His Second Coming).
>
> 1 Peter 1:9–11

In the Old Testament, there are clear predictions of both a suffering servant and of a conquering king. Of course, we know that the Jews of Jesus' day overlooked those predictions of the suffering servant causing them to reject the king from heaven on that dark day in which he died for the sins of the world!

In this section, let's look at some of the many wonderful words that speak of our Lord's first coming, words that he no doubt shared with those two men on the road to Emmaus. But first, let us remind ourselves how God feels about his prophetic word.

Behold, the former things are come to pass, and new things do I declare: Before they spring forth I tell you of them.

Isaiah 42:9

Remember the former things of old: For I am God, and there is none else; I am God, and there is none like me. Declaring the end from the beginning, and from ancient times the things that are not yet done, saying, My counsel shall stand, and I will do all my pleasure.

Isaiah 46:9–10

Truly, God uses prophecy to show us that he is God, and there is none else. There is none like him!

For further study:

1. God uses prophecy to reveal his power. What else does he use? See Psalm 19:1-3 & Isaiah 40:25-26.

2. The Jews, for the most part, missed the prophetic signs of Christ's first coming. Are there any prophetic words in play in our day today which may give insight towards the soon second coming of our Lord?

THE PROTOEVANGELICUM

T HE FIRST MENTION of the Son of God and of the Son of Man is found early in the book of Genesis. After Adam and Eve sinned, God told both of them as well as the serpent of what he was planning to do to remedy the situation. At the time, the prophecy likely seemed to be a bit mystical, but in retrospect, it can be clearly seen as a stirring prophecy of both the first and second comings of Jesus Christ.

> And I will put enmity between thee and the woman, and between thy seed and her seed; it shall bruise thy head, and thou shall bruise his heel.
>
> Genesis 3:15

In speaking to the serpent, God told him that the woman and he would be perpetual enemies. This is so often the way it is. When two individuals are caught up in sin together, they invariably will grow to hate one another.

God told Satan that her seed (the Messiah) would bruise his head. A better translation is that Eve's son, the Son of Man, would crush is head. This of course foretells of that furious day when after defeating the forces of the Antichrist in the Valley of Armageddon, the King of kings will banish the serpent to the bottomless pit called the abyss. Later, that adversary of Eve's children will be cast into the Lake of Fire at the end of the millennial age. Truly, his head will be crushed. But the prophecy does mention an apparent victory by the serpent over the Savior. We are told that the snake will bruise his, the Lord's, heel. On that day, nearly two thousand years ago, Satan mobilized the Romans and the Jews to crucify the promised seed. He believed he had won out, that he had beaten the prophecy, that he had more than bruised Jesus' heel. How insanely incensed he must have been when three days later, the stone was rolled away, and the Lord rose in victory and honor. At that moment, it must have become clear to him. He had lost! Only the end game was left before his ultimate fate would prove to be a reality!

For further study:

1. Do you think that the fear of snakes has its origins in the curse of Genesis 3:15?

2. Have you ever been caught up in sin with another person? How well do you two get along now? What did you do, or can you do, to remedy the feelings you had or hold towards that person?

3. Genesis 3:15 implies that the serpent has seed, i.e. children. Who are these children of the serpent?

THE GENERATIONS
OF ADAM

HIDDEN IN THE Bible to those who do not speak Hebrew is a wonderful prophecy telling of the Messiah. After speaking of the story of Cain and Abel and learning that a third son was born to our first parents whose name was Seth, we are told of the generations of Adam. That is, we learn of the names and the years of the first son of each of the ten generations that followed after Adam. Of course, there were many, many other sons and daughters born in each generation as people were living long upon the earth in those days, but the story of salvation is given in the Hebrew, meaning of the firstborn son's names. Let me show you.

The first born of creation named Adam is the Hebrew word for "man." His surviving son (and thus the bearer of firstborn status) was Seth. His name means "appointed." Seth begot Enos, meaning "subject to death." Enos begot Cainan whose name is interpreted as "sorrowful." Cainan's firstborn son was called Mahalaleel. That name is "from the presence of the Lord." Jared was Mahalaleel's son. Jared means "one comes down." Jared fathered Enoch whose name means "dedicated." At the age of sixty-five, Enoch fathered Methuselah. This patriarch's name means "dying he shall send."

This eldest son of the eighth generation begat Lamech whose name means "to the poor and lowly." Lamech completed the picture God was painting by siring the godly man we know as Noah. Noah's name wonderfully means "rest and comfort."

So putting the names together tells the story. Man, subject to death, sorrowful. From the presence of the Lord, one comes down dedicated. Dying he shall send to the poor and lowly, rest and comfort.

What are the odds of that happening! This, along with so many other things I have written of over the years, continues to bless me with the realization that this book, which we hold in our hands is truly a masterpiece written by the finger of God!

For further study:

1. Why is Jesus such rest & comfort to you?

2. What happened to the first son of the seventh generation? How is the meaning of his name related to what happened to him?

3. In calculating the ages of Methuselah & Lamech from Genesis 5 as well as knowing from Genesis 8:13 that Noah was six hundred years old when the Flood occurred, where these two forefathers of Noah killed in the Flood?

THE SEED OF ABRAHAM

Now the Lord had said to Abram, Get thee out of thy country (Southern Iraq today), and from thy kindred, and from thy father's house, unto the land that I will show thee: And I will make of thee a great nation, and I will bless thee...and in thee shall all of the families of the earth be blessed.

Genesis 12:1–3

BEFORE ABRAM EVEN knew the Almighty God, before he had become the one called "the father of faith," Abram was called out by God's grace and providence for greatness. And not only did God tell Abram that he would be the father of a great nation (Israel), but he also told Abram that in him, all families of the earth would be blessed.

How was that to be?

And in thy seed shall all the nations of the earth be blessed.

Genesis 22:18

This amplified revelation tells that in and by Abraham's seed, all of mankind, not just Israel would be forever blessed.

Now the New Testament of course gives the fulfillment of these prophecies. We know that Jesus Christ is the promised seed of Abraham, and that in dying, he purchased the way of salvation for all nations. Matthew 1:1–16 gives the genealogy of Jesus from Abraham, showing that the Lord does indeed meet the lineage requirement of messiah by being a direct descendant of Abraham. Peter and Paul independently speak of the actual prophetic fulfillment of the Genesis promises. First, in Peter's day of Pentecost evangelistic explanation of the outpouring of the Holy Spirit, he sums up the message of Jesus Christ and him crucified by saying,

> Ye are the children of the prophets, and of the covenant which God made with our fathers, saying unto Abraham, And in thy seed shall all the kindreds of the earth be blessed. Unto you first God, having raised up his Son Jesus, sent him to bless you, in turning away every one of you from his iniquities.

Acts 3:25–26

Next, Paul speaking to the Galatians of faith in Jesus Christ, the promised seed of Abraham, states.

> And the scripture, foreseeing that God would justify the heathen through faith, preached before the gospel unto Abraham, saying, In thee shall all nations be blessed.

Galatians 3:8

Truly, it is in Abraham's seed, Jesus Christ, the one who has conquered death, that all of mankind has been blessed with an unimaginable gift!

For further study:

1. According to Matthew 1:17, how many generations are there from Abraham to Christ? Is that number biblically significant? Why?

2. Abraham lived over two thousand years before Christ. Do you think God seemly delays fulfilling his promises? Why or why not?

PSALMS SINGING OF JESUS

THE NEW TESTAMENT writers, in speaking of Jesus, quoted the Psalms more than any other book. Could it be that an oral tradition was begun on the road to Emmaus, which later was transcribed into written form? I think it very likely.

PSALM 8

What is man that thou art mindful of him? And the son of man that thou visitest him? For thou has made him a little lower than the angels, and hast crowned him with glory and honor. Thou madest him to have dominion over the works of thy hands; thou hast put all things under his feet.

Psalms 8:4–6

Theses verses seem to be speaking of Israel's son, the Son of Man. This title, also found in Ezekiel and Daniel, was a favorite of our Lord's when speaking in the third person of himself.

We find the fulfillment documented in the book to the Hebrews.

> But one in a certain place testified, saying, what is man, that thou art mindful of him? Or the son of man, that thou visitest him? Thou madest him a little lower than the angels; Thou crowned him with glory and honor, and didst set him over the works of thy hands: Thou hast put all things in subjection under his feet...we see Jesus, who was made a little lower than the angels for the suffering of death, crowned with glory and honor: That he by the grace of God might taste death for every man.
>
> Hebrews 2:6–9

Jesus, being made a little lower than the angels, how can that be?

Amplification of this idea is found in Paul's letter to the believers in Philippi.

> Who being in the form of God, thought it not robbery to be equal with God: But made himself of no reputation, and took upon him the form of a servant, and was made in the likeness of men: And being found in the fashion of a man, he humbled himself, and became obedient unto death, even the death of the cross.
>
> Philippians 2:6–8

Truly, Jesus, the only obedient one, the Son of Man, tasted death for every man, so that we might live! What a Savior we have!

PSALM 22

This powerful psalm has been called the crucifixion psalm. Written one thousand years before Christ's death and hundreds of years before this form of capital punishment was even devised. It eerily predicted what the redeemer would suffer to clear our name. Of course, the New Testament writers quote this psalm frequently in speaking of Lamb of God. I long for the day when the Jews, the people of the composer David, will see that this psalm sings of Jesus.

> My God, my God, why hast thou forsaken me? But I am a worm and no man; a reproach of men, and despised of the people. All that see me laugh me to scorn: They shoot out their lips, they shake the head, saying, He trusted on the Lord that he would deliver him: Let him deliver him, seeing he delighted in him...Many bulls have compassed me: Strong bulls of Bashan have beset me round. They gaped upon me with their mouths, as a ravening and roaring lion. I am poured out like water, and all my bones are out of joint: My heart is like wax; it is melted in the midst of my bowels (chest). My strength is dried up like a potsherd; and my tongue cleaveth to my jaws...For dogs have compassed me: The assembly of the wicked have enclosed me: They pierced my hands and my feet. I may tell all my bones: They look and stare at me. They part my garments among them, and cast lots upon my vesture.
>
> Psalm 22:1–18 (excerpts)

The first verse has always been the key for the Jews. "My God, my God, why hast thou forsaken me?" I am told that rabbis, even to this day, will call their students to a portion of scripture by quoting the first verse of the section they want to discuss. So picture the scene, the rabbi from Nazareth was in the process of certain death, yet he calls the observers to consider Psalm 22 by quoting the first verse. Brilliant! This must have stopped the mouths of those with eyes to see on that day!

The phrase "I am a worm" is also very significant. The worm spoken of here was common to Israel called a Tola. The tola is a red worm that in order to reproduce would climb a tree, deliver wormy babies under her, and then die. She would turn white on the third day and flake off the tree! Doesn't take much to see what the Tola, Jesus Christ, did in this analogy of David's.

Next, the bulls of Bashan speak of the demonic entities, which were taunting our Lord as he hung on the cross. Peter in his epistle calls Satan a roaring lion, similar to the description given here by David!

The actual medical details involved in death by crucifixion are poignantly described. Dislocated joints, congestive heart failure, and terrible thirst were predicted for our Savior! Think with me on this, Jesus knew about Psalm 22. How sobering it is to consider that he knew it spoke of him!

Lastly, among many other points that could be made about this powerful section of scripture, are the words, "Dogs have compassed me." Dogs in the Old Testament often speak of the Gentiles. Truly, the gentile soldiers were surrounding Jesus. They pierced his hands and feet. They could see all of his bones as he sucked tortuously for each breath. They parted his garments, and they cast lots for his vesture.

PSALM 31

Luke in his gospel informs us that Jesus quoted a second psalm, which he wanted to direct his listeners to as they considered his sacrifice.

> And when Jesus had cried with a loud voice, he said, Father, into thy hands I commend my spirit.
>
> Luke 23:46

This quote is the key verse of Psalm 31.

> Into thine hand I commit my spirit: Thou hast redeemed me, O Lord God of truth.
>
> Psalm 31:5

Psalm 31 was a Hebrew bedtime story memorized by all the Jews of Jesus' day. It speaks of God's deliverance after the men of Keyila let David down in betraying him to King Saul. Jesus was telling his listeners, and all by extension, that God will deliver him just as he delivered David. Three days later, this was fulfilled. The earth quaked, and the stone rolled away!

PSALM 41

Written by David, this psalm speaks of God's deliverance toward him after the coup masterminded by David's son Absalom and his trusted advisor Ahithophel. Specifically, the latter was in David's inner circle yet secretly partnered with Absalom in an effort to take David out. David sang,

> Yea, mine own familiar friend, in whom I trusted, which did eat of my bread, hath lifted up his heel against me.
>
> Psalm 41:9

On the night he was betrayed, Jesus told his disciples that this psalm also spoke of what would happen to him.

> I speak not to you all: I know whom I have chosen: But that the scripture may be fulfilled, He that eateth bread with me hath lifted up his heal against me. Now I tell you before it come, that, when it is come to pass, ye may believe that I am.
>
> John 13:18–19

PSALM 45

The book of Hebrews documents that Psalm 45 speaks not only of King David but, more importantly, of Christ. On the road to Emmaus, the Lord likely pointed this out.

> But unto the Son he saith, Thy throne, O God, is forever
> and ever: A scepter of righteousness is the scepter of thy
> kingdom. Thou has loved righteousness and hated iniq-
> uity; Therefore God, even thy God, hath anointed thee
> with the oil of gladness above thy fellows.

> Hebrews 1:8–9

Indeed, Jesus was the man of sorrows as the iniquities of us all were taken by him (Isaiah 53), but he also is anointed with the oil of gladness due to his hatred of sin! Truly holiness equals happiness. Strive after it, dear saint, and you too will have joy!

PSALM 68

This wonderful section prophesies of the gifts of the Holy Spirit that we body of believers would receive after our Lord's completed sacrifice.

> Thou hast ascended on high, thou hast led captivity cap-
> tive: Thou hast received gifts for men...Blessed be the
> Lord, who daily loaded us with his benefits, even the God
> of our salvation.

> Psalm 68:18–19

We find the fulfillment of these words in Paul's letter to the Ephesians.

> But unto every one of us is given grace according to the
> measure of the gift of Christ. Wherefore he saith, when
> he ascended up on high, he led captivity captive, and gave
> gifts unto men...And he gave some apostles; and some,
> prophets; and some, evangelists; and some, pastors and
> teachers; for the perfecting of the saints, for the work of
> the ministry, for the edifying of the body of Christ.

> Ephesians 4:7–8, 11–12

After freeing us from our sins (taking captivity captive), Jesus gave gifts unto men (the five gift ministries of the church). The mercy and grace of God are seen in this prophecy. The judgment we deserve is withheld (mercy), and the benefits we don't deserve is bestowed (grace)!

PSALM 69

Another psalm of David powerfully speaks of Christ. The first twenty-one verses tell of our Lord's first advent and the remaining verses speak of his second coming. Interestingly this psalm is quoted seven times in the New Testament.

Here are a few excerpts that Jesus may have reminded those men as they traveled to Emmaus.

> Save me, O God...I sink in deep mire, where there is no standing...my throat is dried...They that hate me without cause are more than the hairs of mine head: They that would destroy me, being mine enemies wrongfully, are mighty...Because for thy sake I have borne reproach; shame has covered my face. I am become a stranger to my brethren, an alien to my mother's children. For zeal of thine house hath eaten me up; and the reproaches of them that reproached thee are fallen on me...Reproach hath broken my heart; I am full of heaviness: And I looked for some to take pity, but there was none; and for comforters, but I found none. They gave me gall for my meat; and in my thirst they gave me vinegar to drink.
>
> Psalm 69:1–4, 7–9, 20–21

Like Psalm 22, Psalm 69 written hundreds of years before the fact, tells of Jesus' sacrifice for you and me!

PSALM 78

I will open my mouth in a parable: I will utter dark sayings of old (Psalm 78:2)

This teaching psalm of the priest Asaph described Israel's rescue and pilgrimage and is a picture of our salvation and walk in this life before we reached the promised land of heaven. Significantly, Matthew quoted this psalm in speaking of our Lord's teaching ministry to the Jews.

> Another parable spake he unto them; The kingdom of heaven is like unto leaven, which a woman took and hid in three measures of meal, till the whole be leavened. All theses things spake Jesus unto the multitude in parables; and without a parable spake he not unto them: That it might be fulfilled which was spoken by the prophet, saying, I will open my mouth in parables; I will utter things which have been kept secret from the foundation of the world.
>
> Matthew 13:33–35

The word parable means "to cast along side." The parable is a wonderful teaching tool used by Jesus to tell of truths in a way that would evoke emotion, require contemplation, and promote the remembrance of that truth in a way that just coming out and plainly saying a truth would not. For instance, which way of telling of the kingdom do you believe is better? "The kingdom of heaven, which I have come to establish, will start out small and slow then grow to infiltrate all of society and culture," or "The kingdom of heaven will be like leaven, which a woman hid, in three measures of meal till the whole be leavened." The first way of teaching this truth can be easily missed and forgotten. The parabolic way forces the seeker to think and remember! Brilliant!

PSALM 118

Tradition teaches that Jesus likely sang this psalm with his disciples at that last Passover meal he shared with them before his death. This psalm is prophetic in its entirety, speaking of our Lord's crucifixion and resurrection in the first thirteen verses and his ministry and return in the last section. But there are two verses that will jump out for the student of scripture as they are quoted time and time again, speaking of the Messiah by the New Testament writers.

> The stone which the builders refused is become the head stone of the corner. This is the Lord's doing; it is marvelous in our eyes.
>
> Psalm 118:22–23

The initial context of this passage speaks of the building of the first temple in Solomon's day. The stones for the temple were cut and shaped in the rock quarry below the temple mount so that they were pre-fit and would be ready to be placed in the temple when they arrived on the mount. But as they constructed the temple, it became apparent to the builders that they were missing the cornerstone. Earlier, a large stone had come up from the quarry for which the builders could not find a place. Thus, they rolled it down the hill not realizing that it was the corner stone upon which all the other stones were to be aligned. In Psalm 118, the psalmist used this powerful imagery from Israel's recent past to speak of the Messiah's ministry.

Jesus of course understood this connection to him, and he quoted this passage to the priests as they were rejecting him during that fateful last week.

> Jesus said to them, Did ye never read in the scriptures, The stone which the builders rejected, the same is become the head of the corner: This is the Lord's doing, and it is marvelous in our eyes?
>
> Matthew 21:42–43

Now picture the context of these powerful words. Jesus had entered into the city riding upon a colt the day prior in an obvious fulfillment of a Messianic prediction given by Zechariah the prophet (Zechariah 9:9). The priests were incensed by this and demanded to know by what authority Jesus was staging this prophetic fulfillment as they were rejecting it as true. Jesus answered by asking a hard question of his own to them. He said that he would say by what authority he was under if they could but answer whether the ministry of John the Baptist was of God or of man. Since the priests had also rejected John, yet the people listening to the exchange revered the prophet, they were reluctant to answer. Then, Jesus spoke in a parable of a father who had two sons and of a householder that planted a vineyard.

Theses two parables spoke of Israel's rejection of the Lord in a way in which they missed. Specifically, the owner of the vineyard (God) sent his servants (the prophets) and his son (the Messiah) to the tenants of the vineyard (the priests of Israel), but they were killed by those men. At the end of his parable, Jesus asked the priests what the owner of the vineyard should do to those evil tenants. Unwittingly, they fell into Jesus' trap and said in unison, "He will miserably destroy those wicked men and will let out his vineyard unto other husbandmen, which shall render him fruits in their seasons" (Matthew 21:41). At that, with a gleam in one eye and a tear in the other, the Messiah quoted the psalmist powerfully indicting them for their rejection of him, the one and only cornerstone upon which all of the building is fitly framed (Ephesians 2:20–21).

Also in the context in Israel's rejection of our Lord on that Palm Sunday weekend, you may remember Jesus' reaction found in the gospel of Luke as the procession came near the city.

> And when he was come near, he beheld the city, and wept over it, Saying, If thou hadst known, even thou, at least in this thy day, the things which belong to thy peace! But now they are hid from thine eyes. For the days shall come

upon thee, that thine enemies shall cast a trench about
thee, and compass thee round, and keep thee on every side,
And shall lay thee even with the ground, and thy children within thee; and shall not leave in thee one stone
upon another; because thou knowest not the time of thy
visitation.

Luke 19:41–44

Jesus wept as he told those listeners, who on that very day,
the things which belong to their peace was upon them. Yet the
prophet foresaw that the learned of the nation had not understood. They had not perceived that for which they should have
comprehended and, thus, in their rejection of their peace, the
prince of peace, they would bring terrible judgment upon themselves even to the destruction of their temple, their city, and
their nation!

But the question must be raised. How should the leaders have
known that this was the day of their visitation?

The answer to which our Lord was alluding to is found in one
of the greatest and well-known sections of the Hebrew scripture,
the book of Daniel.

Know therefore and understand, that from the going forth
of the commandment to restore and to build Jerusalem
unto the Messiah the Prince shall be seven weeks, and
threescore and two weeks.

Daniel 9:25

Daniel told the Jews to know therefore and understand. Pay
attention to this. This is going to happen! After the commandment to rebuild Jerusalem was proclaimed until the arrival of
the Messiah, the prince would be sixty-nine weeks. The Jewish
scribes knew from many other scriptures that a week in biblical
prophecy was a period of seven years. Thus, Daniel was telling his
people that sixty nine times seven or four hundred eighty-three
years will pass from the commandment to restore and rebuild

Jerusalem until the coronation of the Messiah. That commandment by Cyrus the king of the Medes and Persians occurred on March 14, 445 BC. Taking into account that the Jewish year is three hundred sixty days, not the 365.25 that we use, three hundred sixty days times four hundred eighty-three years brings us to April 6, AD 32. Apparently, according to Jesus' own words as documented in Luke's gospel, 4/6/32 was the very day that Daniel's prophecy was realized! The Jews missed it badly, causing Jesus to weep over the city as he was arriving in the coronation procession foretold so many years earlier by the prophet Daniel.

The next three verses of the Psalm 118, prophecy also verify that that Palm Sunday was the day Daniel foresaw.

> This is the day that the Lord hath made; we will rejoice and be glad in it. Save now [Hosanna], I beseech thee, O Lord: O Lord, I beseech thee, send now prosperity. Blessed is he that cometh in the name of the Lord.
>
> Psalm 118:24–26

Of course the fulfillment of these words is seen to all in that Palm Sunday procession.

> And a very great multitude spread their garments in the way; others cut down branches from the trees, and strawed them in the way. And the multitude that went before, and that followed, cried, saying, Hosanna to the Son of David: Blessed is he that cometh in the name of the Lord: Hosanna in the highest.
>
> Matthew 21:8–9

In this, there is a warning to you and me. Today, in our day, we also have scores of prophecies, which are coming to pass before our very eyes in the news of our times. Israel coming back as a nation, earthquakes, pestilences, and famines proceeding forth as birth pangs, oceans raging, and Jerusalem once again becoming a cup of trembling for the nations. We see Iran partnering with

Russia and others in posturing against Israel; the days that we live in are like the days of Noah and Lot. Yes, these are the days prior to our Lord's second coming. Yet the words of Paul, speaking of the world's ignorance of our time is sobering.

> But of the times and the seasons, brethren, ye have no need that I write unto you. For you yourselves know perfectly that the day of the Lord so cometh as a thief in the night. For when they shall say, Peace and safety; then sudden destruction cometh upon them, as travail upon a woman with child; and they shall not escape.
>
> 1 Thessalonians 5:1–3

Just as the Jews in Jesus' day did not understand the time of their visitation, we learn that the days prior to the day of the Lord will also be a surprise to many poor souls. This causes me to weep!

Paul gives words of warning and comfort to those of us given eyes to see as he ends this thought by saying that we believers are not of the darkness that we should be overtaken by the thief. He states that we are children of the light, and thus, he implores us to keep watching (2 Thessalonians 5:4–6).

Look up, little children, for the time of our redemption draweth near!

PSALM 132

As noted above, the believing multitude of Jesus' day did understand that he was not just the son of Mary but the one coming in the name of the Lord was indeed the prophesied Son of David.

> The Lord hath sworn in truth unto David; he will not turn from it; Of the fruit of thy body will I set upon thy throne...There I will make the horn of David to bud: I have ordained a lamp for mine anointed.
>
> Psalm 132:11 and 17

The fulfillment of this prophecy is seen in the New Testament by two who knew of Jesus' true lineage.

First, John the Baptist father Zacharias, after his tongue was loosed, prophesied of the coming son of David.

> Blessed be the Lord God of Israel; for he hath visited and redeemed his people, and hath raised up an horn of salvation for us in the house of his servant David; as he spake by the mouth of his prophets, which have been since the world began.
>
> Luke 1:68–70

Peter, in that great sermon given on the day of Pentecost, also proclaimed Jesus' true heritage.

> For David speaketh concerning him, I foresaw the Lord always before my face...thou wilt not leave my soul in hell [the grave], neither wilt thou suffer thine Holy One to see corruption [decay]...Men and brethren, let me freely speak unto you of the patriarch David, that he is both dead and buried, and his sepulchre is with us unto this day. Therefore being a prophet, and knowing that God had sworn with an oath to him, that of the fruit of his loins, according to the flesh, he would raise up Christ to sit on his throne; He seeing this before spake of the resurrection of Christ, that his soul was not left in hell [the grave], neither did his flesh see corruption.
>
> Acts 2:25, 27, 29–31

The application of this prophecy should be clear. In spiritual life, things are not always as they appear! The Jewish leaders chose to believe that Jesus was a bastard who was conceived out of wedlock and born by a woman from Nazareth, a town in the tribe of Naphtali, far removed from Judah and of the line of David. But obviously, from the Psalm Sunday praises, which we saw earlier, many of the people of Jerusalem understood that Jesus was from

David's line. The Jewish leaders though believed they knew more about Jesus when actually they knew less. This can also happen to you and me. Something in spiritual life or something read in the Bible can be hard to understand, can be confusing and even troubling, and can sometimes even lead to difficult questions and implications about God and his ways. When that happens, and it will as we walk with him, I must never sacrifice the things I know about the Lord on the altar of the things I don't. I must not discard the truths I know about our maker, his love and mercy and grace because of things I cannot comprehend and by which may even be disturbed.

For further study:

1. David penned many of the psalms which prophecy of Christ while in danger and on the run from Saul. How does this painful portion of David's life relate to Paul's words found in 2 Corinthians 4:16-18?

2. Ahithophel betrayed David as Judas did Jesus. What leads a person to betray a trusted friend? 2 Samuel 11:3 & 23:34 reveal that Ahithophel was Bathsheba's grandfather. Do you think it is possible that Ahithophel harbored a root of bitterness (Hebrews 12:15) over David's dealings with Bathsheba's husband Uriah which led him to later betray David when the opportunity presented itself years later during the coup attempt by Absalom?

3. Jesus spoke in parables. Which one is your favorite & why?

4. Do you have a scripture which causes you to stumble in your faith? How should you handle your reaction to that scripture that does not seem to go with the rest of the flow of God's word?

HE SHALL BE
CALLED EMMANUEL

THE PROPHET ISAIAH has in my opinion some of
the most stirring prophecies speaking of the Lord Jesus Christ. It
will be my great pleasure in the next few sections to discuss some
of the wonderful scriptures, which Jesus fulfilled perfectly!

Isaiah, along with his contemporary Micah, was a prophet
whose primary ministry was to the kingdom of Judah. The ten
northern tribes of Israel had succeeded from Judah and Benjamin
two hundred years previously. Although brothers, time had
brought a rift between the two kingdoms and periodic civil wars
occurred in those days as documented in the books of the kings
of Israel and Chronicles.

Early in Isaiah's ministry, the king of Judah was David's great-
great-great-great-great-grandson, Ahaz. This sixth generation
son of David was the first in the line of Judean kings to be cited

as doing evil in the sight of the Lord. Basically, Ahaz was an unbeliever! We see him taking Judah down the road of idolatry in 2 Chronicles, and the Bible has nothing good to say about his reign because of that sin.

Near the beginning in Ahaz's reign, Isaiah was commissioned by God to speak to him about an alliance that Syria and Israel were promoting in an effort to fortify against their common enemy, the up-and-coming kingdom of Assyria. God told Isaiah to warn Ahaz against joining with the heathen nation of Syria and the backsliding kingdom of Israel. He told Ahaz that in sixty-five years, Israel would be broken (which of course did happen as Isaiah predicted), for in 726 BC. Assyria came down and carried away the ten northern tribes into captivity. The Lord then told Ahaz to ask for a sign that this prophecy was indeed going to be fulfilled. To that, Ahaz told Isaiah that he would not tempt the Lord in asking for such a sign. In response to Ahaz's hypocrisy, Isaiah stirringly replied,

> Hear ye now, O house of David; Is it a small thing for you to weary men, but will ye weary my God also? Therefore the Lord himself shall give you a sign, Behold, a virgin shall conceive, and bear a son, and shall call his name Immanuel.
>
> Isaiah 7:13–14

His name shall be called Emmanuel, or more correctly, his name will mean Emmanuel, that is "God with us." Truly, as Isaiah predicted, the Lord *Himself,* Jesus the second person of the mysterious Trinity was himself the sign given. He is Emmanuel, God with us!

We also see something else almost as remarkable as God becoming a man, and that is, that a virgin would conceive. In 780 BC, people did not know about the sperm and the egg coming together in the conception process, but everyone did understand that virgins did not have children. The act of intimacy was well understood to somehow lead to conception, and thus, a virgin would be totally excluded from any possibility of childbearing.

But in Matthew's gospel, we find corroboration of this unique event from no less of an authority but the angel of the Lord!

> But while he [Joseph] thought on these things, behold, the angel of the Lord appeared to him in a dream, saying, Joseph, thou son of David, fear not to take unto thee Mary thy wife: For that which is conceived in her is of the Holy Ghost...Now all of this was done, that it might be fulfilled which was spoken of the Lord by the prophet [Isaiah], saying, Behold, a virgin shall be with child, and they shall call his name Emmanuel, which being interpreted is, God with us.
>
> Matthew 1:20, 22–23

The virgin birth happened only one time in history, reserved only for the Messiah, the Son of God! How cool is that!

As an aside, before we move to another wonderful prophecy of Isaiah, we see in this story a principle of God that is important to acknowledge. That is, God's promises will happen whether I believe them or not! For instance, when the Lord tells me though his word that he will never leave me or forsake me, I can choose to believe that in all circumstances or not. But my unbelief doesn't change the fact that he will never leave or forsake me. I just miss out on the peace and the blessing because of my lack of faith! Don't let that happen to you, dear reader. We have precious promises given to us by our maker. He is more than able to come through. After all, if he can cause a virgin to conceive, taking care of my problems, large or small, is no big thing to a power of that magnitude!

For further study:

1. What has God promised and performed for you lately despite your unbelief?

2. Joseph & Mary both believed the impossible had happened, that of a virgin conceiving. How does one get that sort of faith?

3. Is the doctrine of the Trinity easy for you to understand? Can you put it into words?

I SAW THE LORD SEATED
ON HIS THRONE

D O YOU KNOW what a Christophany is? We alluded to one when we studied Joshua, the captain of the Lord's host. You see a Christophany is an appearance of the Lord Jesus to someone in the Old Testament before he arrived on the scene as the babe from Bethlehem. Jesus was the captain who told Joshua to take off his shoes as the ground he was standing upon was holy. Other examples include the visit to Abraham of the three men informing that patriarch that his nephew Lot's home of Sodom was soon to be destroyed. Jesus and two angels were in that party. As you may remember, the two angels then traveled to Sodom and protected Lot as the prophecy concluded. The angel of the Lord (Jesus) appeared to Sampson's mother and father in delivering the news of the soon conception of that mighty judge of Israel. From the context, it is clear that the messenger was no mere angel but God himself! To conclude this concept, as there are numerous other examples, let's look at Jesus' appearance to the prophet Isaiah.

> In the year that king Uzziah died I saw the Lord sitting upon a throne, high and lifted up, and his train filled the temple. Above it stood the seraphims: Each one had six wings; with two he covered his face, and with two he covered his feet, and with two he did fly. And one cried unto another, and said, Holy, holy, holy, is the Lord of hosts: The whole earth is full of his glory. And the posts of the door moved at the voice of him that cried, and the house was filled with smoke.
>
> Isaiah 6:1–4

That was quite a scene! Isaiah saw the Lord. He saw the Almighty. He saw the holy one! Look at his response,

> Then said I, Woe is me! For I am undone; because I am a man of unclean lips, and I dwell in the midst of a people of unclean lips: For mine eyes have seen the King, the Lord of hosts.
>
> Isaiah 6:5

Isaiah was undone! He realized his imperfection acutely as he gazed upon the truth and the light!

Next, the Lord demonstrated how fire from the altar of sacrifice would cleanse Isaiah from sin.

> Then flew one of the seraphims unto me, having a live coal in his hand, which he had taken with the tongs from off the altar: And he laid it upon my mouth, and said, Lo, this hath touched thy lips; and thine iniquity is taken away, and thy sin purged.
>
> Isaiah 6:6–7

The imagery here is so cool! It's a picture of the new birth! The live coal from the altar touching his lips speaks of the fire of God's wrath coming from the altar of sacrifice and of confession to that truth by a man or woman. For the Bible clearly states that we must confess with our mouths in order to be saved (Romans 10:9).

Next, we learn of Isaiah's commission.

> Also I heard the voice of the Lord, saying, Whom shall I send, and who will go for us? Then said I, Here I am; send me.
>
> Isaiah 6:8

No wonder Isaiah was so great! The great God, Elohim, the multifaceted God who asked, "Who will go for us," received a ready response from his man Isaiah. Lord, I pray that I would be like that!

> And he said, Go, and tell this people, Hear ye indeed, but understand not; and see ye indeed, but perceive not. Make the heart of this people fat, and make their ears heavy, and shut their eyes; lest they see with their eyes, and hear with their ears, and understand with their heart, and convert, and be healed.
>
> Isaiah 6:9–10

God told Isaiah to speak the word knowing that the people were hardened to it and would not receive. That way, later when they did wake up out of their spiritual stupor, they could not blame God for abandoning them. This is always the way with God. Whether it is Israel or America, whether it is Jehoshaphat or the president, whether it is you or me, God will warn us before we walk off the cliff of carnality and idolatry. The question is, do we hear, do we see, do we perceive? Often, the answer from mankind to the maker is no!

So Isaiah saw Jesus in the year that king Uzziah died (verse 1). How do I know it was Jesus, and not the Father? John's gospel makes that question clear.

> This he (Jesus) said, signifying what death he should die. The people answered him, We have heard out of the law that Christ abideth for ever: How sayest thou, the Son of Man must be lifted up (die)? Who is this Son of Man?
>
> John 12:33–34

The people here are clearly demonstrating their prophesied lack of understanding. From their scriptures in Isaiah, Ezekiel, and Daniel it is clear that the Messiah would suffer and die and that he is called the Son of Man!

> Then Jesus said unto them, Yet a little while is the light with you. Walk while ye have the light, lest darkness come upon you: For he that walkest in darkness knoweth not whither he goeth...These things spake Jesus, and departed...But though he had done so many miracles before them, yet they believed not on him: That the saying of Isaiah the prophet might be fulfilled...He hath blinded their eyes, and hardened their heart; that they should not see with their eyes, nor understand with their heart, and be converted, and I should heal them. These things said Isaiah when he saw his glory, and spake of him.
>
> John 12:35–38, 40–41

Whose glory did Isaiah see? Why the subject of this conversation is Jesus not the Father. The Word clearly teaches here that Isaiah saw the Lord High and lifted up. Isaiah saw Jesus. Isaiah witnessed a Christophany! Certainly, Jesus may have mentioned these scriptures to those two men on the road to Emmaus.

Now before we leave this section, I have two applications for us to consider. Note with me what Isaiah did when he saw the Lord. He said, Woe is me, I am undone! He realized that he was so inferior to the Lord that he felt naked and ashamed. When we read in Isaiah before his vision, we hear of condemnation and of disgust in his message. No longer is that the tenor after he saw Jesus! From then on, Isaiah's words contain grace and mercy. They proclaim love, forgiveness, and hope. And that's the point! When I am doling out harsh words to people, words of condemnation and despair, I'm not really seeing the Lord. Jesus is the gracious one, and his wisdom is pure and peaceable, gentle and easy to be entreated, full of mercy and good fruit without partiality and hypocrisy (James 3:17).

Secondly, Isaiah saw the Lord in the year that king Uzziah died. In this little tidbit is embedded a truth. King Uzziah was a great king. In reading his story, God has much praise for this descendant of David. Also, Hebrew scholars teach that Isaiah was likely a close relative to King Uzziah. They were friends. They were confidants. They relied upon each other. But the thing to note is that Isaiah saw the Lord *after* Uzziah was no longer in his life. Could it be that Uzziah, while he was alive, was filling the place in Isaiah's life that was reserved for the Lord? Could it be that after King Uzziah died that Isaiah was able to see the Lord more clearly? I think that is a message that can be gleaned and an application for you and me. Do we have some pastor or preacher, some spiritual leader, or charismatic figure that is taking the place of our redeemer? If so, that person may have to figuratively die in our lives in order for us to see the Lord high and lifted up. Don't be surprised if this happens when we give some fallible human the place that only God can inhabit.

For further study:

1. Is your pastor someone your church cannot do without? Do you have anyone in your life you have elevated
   too high?

2. Why do you envision the seraphims have six wings? Why are two covering their faces & two covering their feet?

3. Why did the seraphims shout Holy, Holy, Holy, is the Lord of hosts? What does it mean to be holy?

4. How does Isaiah 6:9-10 correlate with the parable of the sower & the seed?

THE PEOPLE HAVE SEEN
A GREAT LIGHT

GOD IN HIS word clearly indicated that the ten northern tribes of the nation of Israel would suffer greatly due to their
rejection of him in the Old Testament. They were overrun by the
Assyrians and scattered into the nations even to this day. The resid-
ual of the people were intermixed with the Gentiles to produce
a faction of people called the Samaritans, who lived in the area
we know today as the West Bank. Another ethnic group labeled
the Galileans lived still farther to the north. The Samaritans and
Galileans were half-Jews, if you will. Thus, the Judeans of Jesus'
day looked down upon them as inferior and unredeemable.

So with this background, we see Yeshua enter the scene! True
to his nature, our wonderful Lord went to the outcasts of Israel.
True to his word, Jesus went to find the lost sheep.

> Nevertheless...the land of Zebulon and the land of Naphtali...by way of the sea, beyond Jordan, in Galilee of the nations. The people that walked in darkness have seen a great light: They that dwell in the land of the shadow of death, upon them the light hath shined...For unto us a child is born, unto us a son is given.
>
> Isaiah 9:1, 2 and 6

> Now when Jesus had heard that John was cast into prison, he departed into Galilee; and leaving Nazareth, he came and dwelt in Capernaum, which is upon the sea cost, in the borders of Zebulon and Naphtali: That it might be fulfilled which was spoken by Isaiah the prophet, saying, the land of Zebulon and the land of Naphtali, by way of the sea, beyond Jordan, Galilee of the Gentiles; The people which sat in darkness saw great light, and to them which sat in the region of the shadow of death light is sprung up.
>
> Matthew 4:12–16

This still happens today! Jesus is the light of the world. Without him, things in life are dark and confusing. But when the Lord by his Spirit approaches the heart of every man, a great light will shine. The question of course is the same as with Galilee of the nations. Will a man or a woman see the light? A person must choose to awake from sleep and open their eyes in order to see the morning light. Likewise, by faith, a lost sheep must also open his eyes in order to see the great light!

> That is, the word of faith, which we preach; That if thou shalt confess with thy mouth, the Lord Jesus, and shalt believe in thine heart that God hath raised him from the dead, thou shalt be saved...So then faith cometh by hearing, and hearing by the word of God.
>
> Romans 10:8, 9 and 17

For further study:

1. Do you feel Romans 10:9 is a formula for salvation? What does it say must be done?

2. Does Satan believe Jesus rose from the dead? Why can someone who acknowledges that the resurrection of Christ may have happened still not be saved?

3. Do you feel an audible profession of your faith to be important? Do others know that you believe that Jesus is Lord?

THE SPIRIT OF THE LORD SHALL REST UPON HIM

AS HAS BEEN discussed earlier, the believing Jews of Jesus' day understood him to be the son of David. But God in his word gives us more information concerning the son of David when he also associates Jesus with David's father, Jesse, and when he describes the nature of the Savior's heart.

> And there shall come forth a rod out of the stem of Jesse, and a Branch shall grow out of his roots: And the spirit of the Lord shall rest upon him, the spirit of wisdom and understanding, the spirit of counsel and might, the spirit of knowledge and of the fear of the Lord.
>
> Isaiah 11:1–2

John the Baptist gave confirmation of the spirit, which was upon Jesus with these wonderful words.

242   DANIEL TOMLINSON, M.D.

He that cometh from heaven is above all. And what he hath seen and heard, that he testifieth…He that hath received his testimony hath set to his seal that God is true. For he whom God hath sent speaketh the words of God: *For God giveth not the Spirit by measure unto him.* (emphasis mine)

John 3:31–34

Indeed, there is no limit to the Spirit which is in Jesus. He is complete. He is whole. He is holy!

And the cool thing about knowing one with this kind of spiritual insight is that I too can tap into this. When I need wisdom and understanding, I can find it in Jesus. When I need strength for the day, it's in the Lord. When I desire counsel and knowledge, I can go to the teacher. As Paul so aptly proclaimed, "O wretched man that I am! Who shall deliver me from this body of this death? I thank God through Jesus Christ our Lord" (Romans 7:24–25). He did not say, "How shall I be delivered," but "Who shall deliver?" Dear believer in Jesus, it's never when, where, why, or how, but it is always who! It's always Jesus, for God giveth not the Spirit by measure unto him!

For further study:

1. Check out the four times the word "Branch" with a capital "B" is used in the King James Version of the Bible. Who does that word always speak of?

2. Compare Isaiah 11:1-2 with 1 Corinthians 12:7-10. What do you see?

A Voice Crying in the Wilderness

As we have discussed previously, the prophets of old had to search what the Spirit was revealing when he testified beforehand of the sufferings of Christ and the glory that should follow (1 Peter 1:11). That is, prophecies of both the suffering servant and the conquering king were often intermingled in their writings. This is the case when we consider Isaiah's prophecy concerning the forerunner to the Messiah.

> The voice of him that crieth in the wilderness, Prepare ye the way of the Lord, make straight in the desert a highway for our God.
>
> Isaiah 40:3

> Every valley shall be exalted, and every mountain and hill shall be made low: And the crooked shall be made

straight, and the rough places plain: And the glory of the Lord shall be revealed, and all flesh shall see it together: For the mouth of the Lord hath spoken it.

Isaiah 40:4–5

All four of the gospel writers quote Isaiah 40:3 as being fulfilled in the arrival and ministry of John the Baptist (Mt 3:3, Mk 1:3, Lk 3:4–6, Jn 1:23). Yet, only Luke adds Isaiah 40:4–5 as being included John's ministry. This seems curious to me as those latter two verses speak of the conquering king. They speak of a time when the Lord's glory will be seen and known by all mankind. They speak of a time-still future. So why are they included by Luke in his inspired words? Is there a mistake in God's word?

Well, an authority no less the Jesus himself would not agree with that assumption. After John had been imprisoned by Herod, he commissioned his followers to ask Jesus if he was the one to come or should they look to another. John was sort of in a season of despair and depression as he was now on the sideline, so to speak, in Herod's prison. Jesus told John's disciples to quote the words of Isaiah to him. Jesus said,

Go and show John again those things which ye do hear and see: The blind receive their sight, and the lame walk, the lepers are cleansed, and the deaf hear, the dead are raised up, and the poor have the gospel preached to them.

Matthew 11:4–5

Jesus quoted Isaiah 35:5–6 as being fulfilled in his healing ministry of that day. After John's disciples left to go back to their master, Jesus praised John, stating that no prophet up until that day was greater than the one who came wearing camel hair and eating locusts and wild honey. He then interestingly associated John's ministry with that of that other great Old Testament prophet who also was sort of wild and hairy, that being the prophet, Elijah. Jesus said, "If ye will receive it, this [John] is

Elijah, which was for to come. He who hath ears to hear, let him hear" (Matthew 11:14–15).

This is important as Elijah, by name, was quoted in the Old Testament as coming on the scene prior to the arrival of the Messiah. Let me show you.

> Behold, I will send my messenger, and he shall prepare the way before me...Behold, I will send you Elijah the prophet before the coming.
>
> Malachi 3:1 and 4:5

So is John the Baptist, Elijah the prophet? Well, not exactly. Look further at Malachi's prophecy. Malachi 3:1 is followed by these words,

> And the Lord, whom ye seek, shall suddenly come to his temple...But who may abide the day of his coming? And who shall stand when he appeareth? For he is like a refiner's fire, and like fullers soap.
>
> Malachi 3:1b-2

And Malachi 4:5 ends by saying that Elijah will be sent before the coming "of the great and dreadful day of the Lord" (Malachi 4:5b).

Certainly, Elijah is going to come onto the scene prior to Jesus' second coming. Prior to the day that the Lord's return will be like a refiner's fire and like fuller's soap. Elijah will come prior to that dreadful day when the revelation tells us that blood will flow up to the level of the horse's bridles (Revelation 14:20).

So John the Baptist and Elijah are indeed different. But their ministry and their spirit is the same. That's why Jesus said, "If you will, John is Elijah" (Matthew 11:14). The prophet was saying that if you have ears to hear, you will understand that they are both forerunners of the Messiah, and they both will come in the same spirit. So in that light, Luke's words speaking of John, which include both first- and second-coming prophecies, can been understood as true!

Most certainly, on the road to Emmaus, Jesus mentioned John the Baptist. He mentioned the voice crying in the wilderness saying prepare ye the way of the Lord!

For further study:

1. Early in John's ministry he proclaimed that Jesus was the lamb of God. But after he was imprisoned by Herod it would seem that his faith wavered a bit as he asked if Jesus was the one or should they look for another. What do you do when you, like John, are disappointed with God? When it is not clear what God is doing and things seem to be going badly? See Matthew 11:6.

2. Do you believe Malachi 4:5 & Revelation 11:3-12 speak of the same event?

The Suffering Servant: Bruised for Our Iniquities

T HE WORDS TO follow hardly need any commentary as they are the backbone of first coming prophecy. To understand Isaiah 53 is to comprehend Jesus and his life's mission statement. "For the Son of man has come to seek and save that which was lost" (Luke 19:10).

> Behold, my servant shall deal prudently, he shall be exalted and extolled, and be very high.
>
> Isaiah 52:13

Indeed, the servant will be exalted and extolled, but the path spoken of here is that of the cross. Using the same word *exalted* in speaking of his death, Jesus said, "If I be lifted up exalted from the earth, I will draw all men unto me. This he said, signifying what death he should die" (John 12:32–33).

> As many were astonished at thee...kings shall shut their mouths at him: For that which had not been told them shall they see; and that which they had not heard shall they consider.
>
> Isaiah 53:14–15

What shall kings consider? Why that one of their own the King of kings and Lord of lords would give his life as a ransom for many! Truly, this is astonishing news. It is incredible news—news that causes me to shut my mouth and bow before him in thanksgiving and awe at his inconceivable sacrifice for me!

> His visage was so marred more than any man, and his form more than the sons of men.
>
> Isaiah 52:14

They covered his head and beat his face taunting him to prophecy who hit him. They crowned him with thorns and whipped him brutally. When Pilate felt the bloodthirsty crowd certainly had seen enough, he paraded Jesus before the mob and said, "Behold the man" (John 19:5). Look what you have done to him. Look at him. He is unrecognizable! Yet what did the people say? "Crucify him! Crucify him; we have no king but Caesar" (John 19:15)!

Continuing, the first verse of the next chapter asks the most important question of all time,

> Who hath believed our report? And to whom is the arm of the Lord revealed?
>
> Isaiah 53:1

The arm of the Lord, that is, the power unto salvation, to whom it is revealed? The answer of course, is to those who will believe. "To them gave he power to become the sons of God, even to them that believe on his name" (John 1:12). Most certainly, the good news is astonishing. It causes kings to shut their mouths in wonder. The news causes me to consider that which is unheard of. But it is true! It really did happen. The God of the universe became one of us and died for the sin of mankind. To those who believe and embrace that juxtaposition, God and death, well, to them is the arm of the Lord revealed!

The next eight verses of this wonderful prophecy of Isaiah's give the minute details of the servant's life and ministry. They give the report that you and I believe. We learn that he will grow up before God as a tender plant for there is no pomp and pride seen in the servant's life. The Bible states that he will come as a root out of dry ground. Indeed, Jesus came at a time of spiritual dryness in the nation. He came four hundred years after the last prophet, Malachi, arose in Israel. He had neither form nor comeliness, no outward beauty that that caused him to be desired. He was despised and rejected of men. He was a man of sorrows for indeed he was acquainted with grief.

Why all this sadness?

> Surely he hath borne our griefs and carried our sorrows: Yet we did esteem him stricken, smitten of God, and afflicted. But he was wounded for our transgressions, he was bruised for our iniquities: The chastisement of our peace was upon him; and with his stripes we are healed.
>
> Isaiah 53:4–5

I cannot even fathom these two verses! This is the doctrine of substitution predicted seven hundred years before it happened! Our chastisement was upon him! He grieved, sorrowed, was stricken and smitten, was afflicted, wounded, and bruised because of our iniquities, not his own! And because of the beating he took, because of his stripes, we are healed. We are spiritually made right. Our sins are forgiven and forgotten! Oh, on that day, when Jesus was talking with those two men on the road to Emmaus, as they came to these two verses, they certainly must have paused and praised the God of heaven as they, like we, consider this implausible truth.

The prophecy continues in detail by revealing that the Savior would be oppressed yet would not open his mouth in defense of his rights. He was to be as a lamb led to the slaughter. The baptist alluded to this truth at the very beginning of his ministry when he said, "Behold, the Lamb of God which taketh away the sins of the world" (John 1:29). Paul called Jesus the Passover lamb when he proclaimed, "For even Christ our Passover is sacrificed for us" (1 Corinthians 5:7). Isaiah persisted by informing us the lamb led to the slaughter would make his grave (be killed) with the wicked yet in death (be entombed) with the rich. Of course, the men understood this as being fulfilled when they witnessed Jesus being crucified between two thieves yet buried in the tomb of the very rich man, Joseph of Arimathea.

Finally, after the servant's humiliation, the prophecy ends with his exaltation and glory.

> Therefore will I divide him a portion with the great, and he shall divide the spoil with the strong; because he hath poured out his soul unto death.
>
> Isaiah 53:12

Here's a grand key to life. If I die, I will live. But if I choose to live, then I die! If I will ever learn this paradoxical truth and stop fighting for my rights, stop demanding my way, stop putting myself first, then I will really live. If I will just trust the Lord to fight my battles, if I will say to him, whatever, Lord, your will be done, then I will live. I pray that for you too!

For further study:

1. Do you believe healings are for today? Does Isaiah 53:4 flow with your answer or do you think it is talking about future healing?

2. Have you ever paid off the debt of another? How does that make you like Jesus?

3. Do you fight for your rights? What is the better way? Do you have a verse or two memorized which can assist you toward that goal?

THIS DAY IS THIS
SCRIPTURE FULFILLED
IN YOUR EARS

IN THE EARLY days of his ministry, Jesus was indeed a celebrity. To use the vernacular of our day, he was a rock star! His fame was proceeding forth as he traveled from village to village in Galilee, teaching with authority and healing by the power of God. People were amazed and awed by this rabbi who seemingly had appeared out of nowhere. So when this holy man everyone was talking about arrived back in his little hometown of Nazareth, the elders of the synagogue were perplexed. Here was one of their own, one from low estate and not felt to be of much potential now acting like a prophet of old. Indeed, they must have been confused and more than a bit skeptical!

With that as a backdrop, let's look at the amazing words, which were spoken,

> And Jesus returned in the power of the Spirit into Galilee: And there went out a fame of him through all the region round about. And he taught in their synagogues being glorified of all. And he came to Nazareth, where he had been brought up: And, as his custom was, he went into the synagogue on the sabbath day, and stood up for to read.
>
> Luke 4:14–16

On the Sabbath, it was customary for adult men, those of age thirty to fifty, to read from the scriptures and then to expound upon the words to those listening. When it came Jesus' turn came to read, he was given the book of Isaiah.

> And when he had opened the book, he found the place where it was written [Jesus knew the Word and knew what he wanted to share]. The Spirit of the Lord is upon me, because he hath anointed me to preach the gospel to the poor; he hath sent me to heal the brokenhearted, to preach deliverance to the captives, and recovery of sight to the blind, to set at liberty them that are bruised, to preach the acceptable year of the Lord.
>
> Luke 4:17–19

Jesus read one-and-a-half verses from today's Old Testament Bible. The words of Luke then say that Jesus closed the book, gave it to the minister, and sat down. With all eyes fastened upon him, the listeners were eager to hear what this rabbi would say about the words he had read.

> Then he began to say to them, "This day is this scripture fulfilled in your ears."
>
> Luke 4:21

Jesus didn't say, "This scripture means such and such." No, he said, today, this very day, the words I am reading to you are fulfilled in my presence. That is, Jesus was clearly stating to those elders and listeners the he, Yeshua of Nazareth, was the anointed one sent by God to preach the gospel to the poor, heal the brokenhearted, preach deliverance to the captives, heal the blind, set at liberty the bruised, and to preach the acceptable year of the Lord. He was clearly proclaiming to those skeptics in his hometown that he was the Messiah!

The story continued by noting that the men of Nazareth did not accept that this "little one" of their own could be the one sent from God for the nation's deliverance, thus, they attempted to kill God's anointed by pushing him off the cliff the village sat upon. Luke implied that it was not Jesus' time to die as he writes that Jesus simply and powerfully walked through the midst of the enraged men as they were powerless to stop this one preaching the acceptable year of the Lord!

But in looking at this section of scripture from Isaiah, the student of the word will note that our Lord stopped right in the middle of the prophecy given by God to Isaiah. After proclaiming the acceptable year of the Lord, the words of Isaiah go on to say, "And the day of vengeance of our God" (Isaiah 61:2).

Jesus stopped where he did because he understood that he was not there on that day to proclaim the day of vengeance of our God. Jesus correctly divided the scriptures as he taught on that Sabbath. He could not have said to those men "this day is this scripture fulfilled in your ears" if he had read that next phrase, as that portion of Isaiah's prophecy was not yet to be fulfilled. We know in hindsight that the day of vengeance of our God is still in the future. Today, we live in the age of grace, awaiting the second coming of the anointed. On that day, a day of awesome fury still in the future, Jesus will physically come back to earth in the clouds with power and great glory. It will be on that day that the final portion of Isaiah's prophecy will be fulfilled. It will be a day that the book of Revelation teaches we will see blood flowing up to the horse's mane in the valley of Armageddon. That will be the day of vengeance of our God upon those who unfortunately do not embrace the one who previously came proclaiming the acceptable day of the Lord!

For further study:

1. Jesus demonstrates 2 Timothy 2:15 very well in this section. Do you agree?

2. Like the men of Nazareth, is it hard for you to spiritually follow someone you have known since childhood, even if they seem anointed by God? Why do you suppose this is true? Is there a way around this problem? See 2 Corinthians 5:16.

OF BLOOD AND WATER: THE NEW COVENANT

WHEN JESUS HUNG on the cross for you and me, he paid the penalty for our sins. He satisfied the payment our sins required by sacrificing himself in our stead. The moment before the Savior died, he said, "It is finished." As he died, the Bible teaches that an earthquake occurred, and the veil in the temple was rent from top to bottom, symbolizing that temple sacrifices were no longer relevant.

Shortly thereafter, the soldiers guarding the crucifixion scene were tasked with killing the three men set to die that day. The Passover was about to begin, and the Jews desired that the bodies be removed before the holy celebration occurred. Pilate ordered the legs of the condemned men to be broken to hasten their deaths. But when the soldiers came to Jesus, they saw that he was already gone, thus, instead of breaking his legs, the centurion pierced our Lord's side with a spear. Remarkably, we are told that out from Jesus' wound came blood and water. These two fluids are the fluids of birth. They are seen together nowhere else in medicine. This shows us Jesus birthed something on that day. Indeed, Jesus birthed in us our salvation. He birthed the new covenant. He birthed forgiveness as pictured by the blood and newness of life in the spirit as typified by the water.

Let's look at the promised new covenant and see how Jesus may have tied it into what had recently happened as he walked with those two men on the road to Emmaus.

> Behold, the days come, saith the Lord, that I will make a new covenant with the house of Israel, and with the house of Judah: Not according to the covenant I made with their fathers in the day that I took them by the hand to bring them out for the land of Egypt; which covenant they brake, although I was an husband to them, saith the Lord: But this shall be the covenant that I will make with the house of Israel: After those days, saith the Lord, I will put my law in their inward parts, and write it in their hearts; I will be their God, and they shall be my people. And they shall teach no more every man his neighbor, and every man his brother, saying, Know the Lord: For they shall all know me, from the least of them unto the greatest of them saith the Lord: For I will forgive their iniquity, and remember their sin no more.
>
> Jeremiah 31:31–34

Jesus spoke of this covenant, and it's relationship to his blood when he spoke these famous words,

> And he took a cup, and when he had given thanks he gave it to them, saying, Drink of it, all of you, for this is my blood of the covenant, which is poured out for many for the forgiveness of sins.
>
> Matthew 26:27–28

Earlier, Jesus spoke of the new covenant's relationship to the water that flowed forth from his wounds and to the Spirit pictured therein with these powerful words,

> In the last day, that great day of the feast, Jesus stood and cried, saying, If any man thirst, let him come unto me, and drink. He that believeth on me, as the scripture hath said, out of his belly shall flow rivers of living water. (But this spake he of the Spirit, which they that believe on him should receive: For the Holy Ghost was not yet given; because that Jesus was not yet glorified.)
>
> John 7:37–39

Also to the woman at the well, our Lord shared,

> Jesus answered and said unto her, If thou knewest the gift of God, and who it is that saith to thee, Give me to drink; thou wouldest have asked of him, and he would have given thee living water...Whosoever drinketh of this water shall thirst again: But whosoever drinketh of that water that I shall give him shall never thirst; but the water that I shall give him shall be a well of water springing up unto everlasting life.
>
> John 4:10, 13–14

Yes, blood and water, forgiveness and grace. It's the new covenant Jesus came to establish!

Jesus explained to his disciples how God will write his word upon our hearts as he taught about the comforter.

> He that believeth on me, the works that I do, shall he do also; and greater works than these shall he do; because I go to my Father...And I will pray the Father, and he shall give you another Comforter, that he may abide with you forever: Even the Spirit of truth...But the Comforter, which is the Holy Ghost, whom the Father will send in my name, he shall teach you all things, and bring all things to your remembrance, whatsoever I have said unto you.
>
> John 14:12, 16–17, 26

Paul spoke of the new covenant's arrival in many places.

> God who has made us sufficient to be ministers of a new covenant, not of the letter [the law of Moses], but of the Spirit. For the letter kills, but the Spirit gives life.
>
> 2 Corinthians 3:6

> But as it is, Christ has obtained a ministry that is much more excellent than the old as the covenant he mediates is better, since it is enacted on better promises. For if that first covenant had been faultless, there would have been no occasion to look for a second. For he finds fault with them when he says: Behold, the days are coming, declares the Lord, when I will establish a new covenant with the house of Israel.
>
> Hebrews 8:6–8

> And every priest stands daily at his service, offering repeatedly the same sacrifices, which can never take away sins. But when Christ had offered for all time a single sacrifice, he sat down at the right hand of God...And the Holy Spirit also bears witness to us; for after saying, This is the covenant that I make with them after those days, declares the Lord: I will put my laws on their hearts, and write them on their minds. Then he adds, I will remember their sins and their lawless deeds no more. Where there is forgiveness of these, there is no longer any offering for sin.
>
> Hebrews 10:16–18

Truly, these words must have burned within the hearts of those men as it does my own, as they considered how great a salvation had been wrought by Jesus' sacrifice and as they looked forward to the soon outpouring of the Spirit.

Indeed, "It is finished!"(John 19:30). Blood and water has poured forth, and we followers of Jesus are the recipients of that wonderful forgiveness and grace.

For further study:

1. Do you think the new covenant, the day the Lord puts his laws in our inward parts, is for today or still in the future?

2. Has the Comforter ever brought to you remembrance of things Jesus has said?

3. When Jesus said from the cross "It is finished" (John 19:30), what did he mean?

THE DAY OF THEIR VISITATION

MUCH LIKE IN our day, the Messiah watch was at a dull roar in first century Israel. People were talking about it. They were excited about it. They wondered if indeed it could be soon. Thus, when John the Baptist arrived on the scene wearing camel skin and eating wild locusts, the question most often asked was "are you the one or do we look for another?" The reason for all the excitement in that day came from an ancient scripture, penned six hundred years earlier by one of their greatest ancestors. The revered prophet Daniel, the prime minister of all Babylon.

> Know therefore and understand, that from the going forth of the command to restore and to build Jerusalem unto the Messiah the Prince shall be seven weeks, and three score and two weeks.
>
> Daniel 9:25

It really couldn't have been any clearer to the Jews. Daniel was told by the angel Gabriel that from the time of the order to rebuild Jerusalem to Messiah would be sixty-nine weeks. To us, this reckoning of time seems unclear but not to the scribe and scholar in Jesus' day. That student of the law understood that a week spoke of a seven-year time frame, much like in our day today a generation speaks of forty years. Examples of a week meaning seven years are many, I'll give you one, and you can look for others if you chose.

After Jacob was tricked by Laban into marrying Leah instead of Rachel, Laban told Jacob "to fulfill her week," and he could marry Rachel also (Genesis 29:27). Jacob understood that to mean that he was to continue to work another seven years for Laban in order to marry both of his daughters.

So back to our story. We find the command to restore and to build Jerusalem in the book of Nehemiah. The year was 445 BC.

> And it came to pass in the month of Nisan [March], in the twentieth year of Artaxeres the king, that wine was before him: And I took up the wine, and gave it unto the king. Now I had not been beforetime sad in his presence. Wherefore the king said unto me, Why is thy countenance sad, seeing that thou are not sick? This is nothing else but sorrow of the heart...Then said I unto the king...why should not my countenance be sad, when the city, the place of my father's sepulchers lieth in waste, and the gates thereof are consumed with fire? Then the king said unto me, For what dost thou make request? So I prayed to the God of heaven and said unto the king, If it please the king, and if thy servant hast found favor in thy sight, that thou wouldest send me unto Judah, unto the city of my fathers sepulchers, that I may build it.
>
> Nehemiah 2:1–5

Nehemiah's request was granted in March of 445 BC, and the time of Daniel's prophecy began. Sixty-nine weeks, or four hundred eighty-three Jewish years later, (the Hebrew calendar has three hundred sixty days), we come to April AD 32. Significantly, this was the month and year our Lord was presented to the nation as the Messiah, the prince. Let's look how it played out.

> Rejoice greatly, O daughter of Zion; shout, O daughter of Jerusalem: Behold, thy King cometh unto thee: He is just, and having salvation; lowly, and riding upon an ass, and upon a colt the foal of an ass.
>
> Zechariah 9:9

Yes, messiah watch was at a fever pitch. The people knew that it was the time. So when the rabbi from Nazareth entered Jerusalem on that fateful Passover week in April AD 32, the people greeted him as Zechariah prophesied they would.

> And when he was come nigh unto Jerusalem...the disciples went and did as Jesus commanded them, and brought the ass, and the colt, and put on them their clothes, and they set him thereon. And a very great multitude spread their garments in the way; others cut down branches from the trees, and strawed them in the way. And the multitudes that went before, and that followed, cried, saying, Hosanna to the Son of David: Blessed is he that cometh in the name of the Lord; Hosanna in the highest.
>
> Matthew 21:1, 6–9

The multitude called him the Son of David, recognizing Jesus as the Messiah. This of course, was not the reception the one having salvation received from the leaders of the nation. They did not call him Lord. They did not accept that he was the fulfillment of Daniel's and Zechariah's prophecies, and this caused our Lord to weep over the repercussions of their unbelief.

> And when he was come near, he beheld the city, and wept over it, saying, If thou hadst known, even thou, at least in this thy day, the things which belong unto thy peace! But now they are hid from thine eyes. For the days shall come

upon thee, that thine enemies shall cast a trench about thee, and compass thee round, and keep thee on every side, and shall lay thee even with the ground, and thy children within thee; and they shall not leave one stone upon another.

Luke 19:41–44

Jesus wept as he understood that on that very day, Daniel's sixty-nine-week prophecy was fulfilled. Yet it was hid by the hardness of their hearts from the spiritual leaders, the ones responsible for the well being of the nation. He foresaw that soon, the city would be leveled so dramatically that not one stone would be left upon another.

Why did this happen?

Because thou knewest not the time of thy visitation.

Luke 19:44

They should have known. The dates were available. Fact is, they did know! They just didn't believe. Like our father, Adam, the fathers of the nation chose to rebel against God, and by their sin of unbelief, they took the children of the nation down to the grave with them.

The next verse of Daniel's sixty-nine-week prophecy tells us that something like that was going to happen.

And...shall Messiah be cut off, but not for himself [it was for our salvation]: And the people of the prince that shall come shall destroy the city and the sanctuary.

Daniel 9:26

Daniel accurately predicted that the Messiah would indeed be rejected, cut off, killed. Subsequently, Daniel added that the people of the prince to come, speaking of the Antichrist, would destroy the city and the temple. All scholars agree that the prince to come will reside over a revived Roman empire. Thus, the people of the prince to come were the Romans. History records clearly that in AD 69, less than a generation after the nation did not recognize the time of their visitation, that the Romans under the command of General Titus leveled the city and burned the temple after a three-year brutal siege. The heat of the fire was so intense that the gold of the temple melted between the stones, causing the spoilers to leave no stone upon another as they grabbed up the golden booty.

Truly the inhabitants of first century Israel were given a unique opportunity, that of witnessing the arrival of the king from heaven. Some understood the times in which they lived, but unfortunately, many others missed it completely.

But what about us in our day today? We too have been given numerous and unmistakable prophetic words that proclaim once again we are living in the time of visitation. Jesus told us to learn the parable of the fig tree. That the generation that witnesses the fig tree (Israel) coming back to life would also see his return. He told us that the times of the second coming would be like the days of Noah and like the days of Lot, days of a population explosion and of celebrated sexual aberrations. Zechariah told us that Jerusalem would be a cup of trembling to all nations in the latter days, and Ezekiel foresaw a coalition of nations led by Russia and Iran coming against Israel at the time of the end.

Lastly, among many more signs I could list, Daniel predicted that in the time proceeding the day of the Lord, people would run to and fro (Hebrew idiom for world travel) and that knowledge would increase.

Could it be any clearer? We, like the Jews of the first century, have been forewarned. The question I have is, "Are you awake?"

> But of the times and the seasons, brethren, ye have no need that I write unto you. For yourselves know perfectly that the day of the Lord so cometh as a thief in the night. For when they shall say, Peace and safety; then sudden destruction cometh upon them, as travail upon a woman

with child; and they shall not escape. But ye, brethren, are not in the darkness, that the day should overtake you as a thief. Ye are children of the light, and the children of the day: We are not of the night, nor of darkness. Therefore let us not sleep, as do others; but let us watch.

1 Thessalonians 5:1–6

Keep watching for his return, fellow children of the light. For the day of our visitation draws near!

For further study:

1. Daniel 9 also speaks of a seventieth week mentioned in verses 23 & 27. What is the seventieth week speaking of?

2. What did Jesus say to the Pharisees, found in Luke 19, when they commanded that he rebuke his disciples for praising him in the way Zechariah had prophesied? How awesome would that have been if it had actually happened!

3. Can you name any prophesies that may be being fulfilled in our day today?

THE FORMER
AND LATTER RAIN

THROUGHOUT HER HISTORY, Israel has been an agricultural nation. Located in the mid-latitudes of our planet with a body of water to the west, she would receive much-needed precipitation for agricultural growing during two seasons of the year when low pressure storm systems would be carried near her. Theses two yearly times were known as the former-and-latter rains. That is, they were the rainy seasons of spring and autumn. During summer, the air was hot and dry as high pressure weather patterns would dominate the land. In winter, low pressure would also bring rain and snow, but of course, the temperatures then were far too cold for agriculture. Thus, the children of Israel were most dependent upon these two rainy seasons. If the land was not prepared by the former rains of spring, then the crop would not sprout forth, and if the latter rains of early autumn were withheld, then the harvest would dry up and die.

The children of Israel understood their dependence upon these two seasonal rainy times, and God promised by his grace to provide these to them.

> I will give you the rain of your land in his due season, the first [former] rain and the latter rain, that thou mayest gather in thy corn, and thy wine, and thine oil.
>
> Deuteronomy 11:14

But when the nation walked away from the Lord, their much-needed rains would cease as a result of their pulling away from his provisions. Cause and effect, one plus one equal two. When the children drifted away, drought and famine was always the repercussion. Case in point, Elijah was able to tell Ahab that a drought was going to come to the land because he understood that the idolatry that Ahab and Jezebel had led the nation into would naturally result the nation moving away from the source of their provision (1 Kings 17 and 18).

Jeremiah explained it to the people with these words.

> Therefore the showers have been withholden, and there hath been no latter rain...thou refused to be ashamed... hast thou seen what backsliding Israel hath done?
>
> Jeremiah 3:3, 6

So the former and latter rains were integral to the life of the nation. They demonstrated God's grace and provision as the people walked with him, and their lack revealed the result of walking away from that place of mercy and abundance. Now I want to be clear about this. God wasn't punishing them in sending a drought when the people would disobey. The dry times were a direct result of their movement, not his! Jude preaches this concept of positional grace with these words, "Keep yourselves in the love of God, looking for the mercy of our Lord Jesus Christ unto eternal life" (Jude 21). The implication of course, is that we must stay under the place where the blessings and grace come forth. If we leave that place of grace and mercy, then we fall prey to calamity and destruction. We move to a position of dryness, drought, and famine. So, this idea of spiritual abundance is clearly seen in the literal times of feast and famine that the children of Israel experienced in the Old Testament. That is, rain and abundance when they were near to God and drought and famine when they were far from their provider.

The same is true in our day today. America, a nation founded on Christian faith and the word of God has received abundance, which surpasses all nations as she has sat under the protection of God and his word. The converse is and will also be true. We can expect more super storms, freak floods, firestorms, and earthquakes as we move away from that place of God's mercy and grace. God is not slamming our country any more than he was slamming Israel. We, like they, are just moving away from him and, thus, leaving his protection. Calamity is always the repercussion of that poor choice!

Now moving on, since the former and latter rains were so important and since they portray such a key spiritual reality, it stands to reason that they would also typify God's most precious gift of all, that of his Son. Indeed they do! On the road to Emmaus, Jesus undoubtedly preached that the former and latter rains are Old Testament pictures of his two visitations to our domain. That is, the former rain picturing the first coming and the latter rain speaking of the second. He likely quoted from the prophets Hosea and Joel to make his point.

> For I will be unto Ephraim as a lion, and as a young lion to the house of Judah: I, even I, will tear and go away; I will take away, and none shall rescue him. I will go and return to my place, till they acknowledge their offense, and seek my face: In their affliction they will seek me early. Come, let us return unto the Lord: For he hath torn, and he will heal us; he hath smitten, and he will bind us up. After two days he will revive us: In the third day he will raise us up,

and we shall live in his sight. Then shall we know, if we follow on to know the Lord: His going forth is prepared as the morning; he shall come unto us as the rain, as the latter and the former rain unto the earth.

Hosea 5:14–6:3

This powerful prophecy, written seven hundred years before Christ, reveals God's entire plan for the salvation of Ephraim and Judah (Israel) in five little verses! The tearing process that began when the nations of Assyria and Babylon were used to chastise Ephraim and Judah respectively was continued by the Romans after the Jews rejected Jesus. The Lord stated that he would go away until they acknowledged their offense. That repentance is still in the future. Early during the tribulation time frame, called the time of Jacob's trouble in Jeremiah 30, the Jews will acknowledge Jehovah as their God, and they will be revived. That will occur after two days. Now the student of the Bible will remember that with the Lord, a day is as a thousand years, and a thousand years is as one day (2 Peter 3:8). Thus, God is proclaiming that the Jews will seek him early in their affliction, two thousand years after he returns to his place (ascended back to heaven), after two days. In the third day, they will be raised up.

Dear believer, we are in the third day! Today, we are living in that day when Israel will be revived, and the Lord will come as the latter rain. On that day, two thousand years ago, the Savior was our former rain.

Speaking the same truth, Joel preaches of the Messianic rain (reign) with these prophetic words.

Be glad then, ye children of Zion, and rejoice in the Lord your God: For he hath given you the former rain moderately, and he will cause to come down for you the rain, the former rain, and the latter rain.

Joel 2:23

Likely, with a rain cloud in the western sky, Jesus and the two men walked toward Emmaus as they considered the rains of Israel and their relationship to God and his ultimate provision!

For further study:

1. Do you think a calamity e.g. Hurricane Katrina, was just something bad that was natural, caused by God because of the people's disobedience or allowed by God but orchestrated by Satan as the people moved away for God's protection?

2. Psalm 90 also has a verse which reveals in God's economy that one day is as a thousand years. Can you find that verse?

3. The term "Jacob's trouble" is found in Jeremiah 30. Read verses 4-11 as well as Deuteronomy 4:29-31 for more information concerning this time.

THE RULER FROM BETHLEHEM

BETHLEHEM, IN THE land of Judah certainly has been one of the most famous cities in the entire world. That is, because we followers of Christ understand that our Savior was born on that Christmas night in Bethlehem! But Bethlehem's fame also preceded the birth of the Messiah two thousand years ago for two other reasons. First, it was the hometown of Israel's great king, David, and secondly, seven hundred years prior to Christ, the prophet Micah foretold that the ruler to come would be born in the little town of Bethlehem.

> But thou, Bethlehem, though thou be little among the thousands of Judah, yet out of thee shall he come forth unto me that is to be ruler in Israel; whose goings forth have been from old, from everlasting.
>
> Micah 5:2

Micah stated that Bethlehem, meaning "house of bread" would be the origin of "the bread from heaven." He prophesied that it would be the birthplace of the Messiah, of the one whose going forth has been from everlasting! Let's look now to the New Testament to see how Christ fulfilled this prophecy. We will see how God moved a mountain, so to speak, in order to have Jesus of Nazareth come to us via Bethlehem.

> And it came to pass in those days, that there went out a decree from Caesar Augustus, that all the world should be taxed...and all went to be taxed, everyone into his own city. And Joseph also went up from Galilee, out of the city of Nazareth, into Judea, unto the city of David, which is called Bethlehem; (because he was of the house and lineage of David) to be taxed with Mary his espoused wife, being great with child. And so it was, that, while they were there, the days were accomplished that she should be delivered.
>
> Luke 2: 1, 3–6

The emperor of the Roman world, the one who was felt to be a God in his own right, believed he was moving the world around at his whim. Little did he comprehend that he was just a puppet in the hands of the Great God who was using his puny proclamation to transport Joseph and Mary to the place he foretold seven hundred years previously! But also, look at this from Joseph and Mary's perspective, she was pregnant, late in gestation no less, and the two of them had to travel forty miles to Bethlehem in order to please the occupying government. What a hassle they must have thought! I'm reminded, of course, in this story of how God's ways as so far above our ways. Often things that seem strange, things that may be difficult and undesired will turn out for a blessing if we just let God work, and let things play out. Indeed, as one of the most famous verses in the Bible states, "All things work together for good to them that love God, to them who are the called according to his purpose" (Romans 8:28).

The Jews of that time understood this prophecy also. Look with me at Matthew's inspired words.

> Now when Jesus was born in Bethlehem of Judea in the days of Herod the king, behold, there came wise men from the east to Jerusalem, Saying, where is he that is born King of the Jews? For we have seen his star in the east, and are come to worship him.
>
> Matthew 2:1–3

This is incredible to me! How did these wise men from the east know that a great king, the Messiah really, had been born when no one in Jerusalem seemingly even had a clue? Well, there is a body of thought in scholastic circles that the ancients had much more knowledge of God than we had previously believed. It is said that the forefathers who descended from Adam through Noah and then through Noah's sons who spread out and repopulated the earth had a rich oral tradition, which among other things, understood that God had written his word in the stars. Of course as the centuries proceeded forth, that knowledge was lost in some groups and bastardized by the occultic science of astrology in others. But living in the east in Jesus' day, it is believed that the wise men, the Magi, where a group of scientists who had retained the original revealed word in the stars, which had come down from the fathers. David confirmed this idea of thought three thousand years after Adam and fifteen hundred years after Noah with this famous song.

> The heavens declare the glory of God; and the firmament showeth his handiwork. Day unto day uttereth speech, and night unto night showeth knowledge. There is no speech nor language, where their voice is not heard.
>
> Psalm 19:1–3

So continuing on with our understanding that the Jews understood where the Messiah would hail from, we see their answer to the magi.

When Herod the king had heard these things, he was troubled, and all Jerusalem with him. And when he had gathered the chief priests and scribes of the people together, he demanded of them where Christ should be born. And they said unto him, In Bethlehem of Judea: For thus it is written by the prophet, And thou Bethlehem, in the land of Juda, art not the least among the princes of Juda: For out of thee shall come a Governor, that shall rule my people Israel.

Matthew 2:4–6

Thinking that the king to come would be born in the capital city, the wise men traveled to Jerusalem and inquired as to his whereabouts. Imagine their surprise when Herod the king, as well as the entire nation, was in the dark about this revelation that was apparently so clear to them. Thus, Herod called for the men who might be able to help, the students of the law, and they correctly headed the Magi in the proper direction. Not in the capitol city, no, go down the road seven miles to a little berg called Bethlehem. It's there that our prophet (Micah) told us that you may find him.

So the wise men went down to Bethlehem and presented Jesus with the gifts of gold, frankincense, and myrrh while Herod plotted how he would handle this threat to his rule. When the Magi failed to return to Herod to give him the report he had desired, he decided to take matters into his own hands. Herod sent a contingent of soldiers down to Bethlehem to kill all of the young boys who were in the age group that was determined by the Magi's timing of the appearance of the star.

Jesus would have been included as a victim in this group had not the angel warned Joseph in a dream to flee south to Egypt in advance of Herod's wicked plans. The Bible states at the end of the story that after Herod had died, it was now safe for Joseph and his family to come back to Israel. But because Herod's evil son Archelaus did reign over Judah, God again warned Joseph to travel back to Nazareth, where he and Mary had originally come from several years previously.

Thus, because of the murderous drama of Jesus' childhood, we have Jesus born in Bethlehem also being called Jesus of Nazareth. Undoubtedly, on the road to Emmaus, Jesus must have shared with those two men that indeed, he was born in Bethlehem, just like Micah had prophesied seven hundred years previously.

For further study:

1. Why according to Romans 8:28 is making friends with your problems a good thing to do?

2. The gifts given to Jesus from the magi were gold, frankincense & myrrh. What do these gifts symbolize?

3. Do you believe the star the magi saw was extremely bright, as depicted in many Christmas presentations, or do you think there was something else about it that alerted the magi while escaping the notice of the masses?

Beauty and Bands: Priced at Thirty Pieces of Silver

THE PROPHET ZECHARIAH came onto the Jewish scene during a time of rival five hundred years before Christ. He is called the prophet of hope as Zechariah's words did raise the eyes of the people up to God in his day. Zechariah received a series of eight visions in one night in the first part of his book followed by a stunning prophecy of the prince coming with salvation in the latter half of his prophetic words. The prophecy of Jesus given in chapters 9–14 detail the entire course of his ministry from his first coming, through the rejection and subsequent scattering of the nation, to the days leading up to the tribulation and his second coming and then on into the millennial time period where the hopeful book ends with the shepherd prince ruling from Jerusalem with the people all living happily ever after!

But in chapter 11, we find the section that our Lord may have shared with those two men on their trip to Emmaus as it directly spoke of the days they had just experienced. Let's take a look.

> And I will feed the flock of slaughter, even you, O poor of the flock. And I took unto me two staves; the one I called Beauty, and the other I called Bands; and I fed the flock.
>
> Zechariah 11:7

Zechariah's parable to the people included some sad news. Here he proclaims that the flock will be fed by a shepherd with two names much like sheep are fattened up before they are led to the slaughter. The two named shepherd of course is the Messiah, the good shepherd, it's Jesus Christ. Jesus is beauty, he is altogether lovely (Song of Solomon 5:16), and he is *bands* or better translated, he is unity as he is the vine to which we are attached. But why would beauty and bands be feeding the flock before they are led to the slaughter? Because of love, because God gave us free will, because we rejected him and wanted our own way.

> Three shepherds also I cut off in one month: and my soul loathed them, and their soul also abhorred me. Then said I, I will not feed you: That that dieth, let it die, and that that is to be cut off, let it be cut off; and let the rest eat every one the flesh of another.
>
> Zechariah 11:8–9

Unfortunately, if we insist upon our own way, God in his love will be forced to let us have it, often to our own detriment. In this case, the three evil shepherds, picturing the leaders of Israel would be cut off in one month after stirring up the people to reject the beautiful shepherd. That month of course occurred in AD 69. when the Romans razed Jerusalem and scattered the Jews including the priesthood.

> And I took my staff, even Beauty, and cut it asunder, that
> I might break my covenant, which I had made with the
> people.
>
> Zechariah 11:10

How sad! God was forced to break his covenant due to the fact that the people abhorred beauty and bands.

Happily, we know the end of the story. God replaced the old covenant with the new covenant fifty days later on the day of Pentecost. On that day the Holy Spirit came upon those who would believe and wrote his will, not upon tablets of stone but upon their hearts!

> And it was broken in that day: And so the poor of the
> flock that waited upon me knew that it was the word of
> the Lord. And I said unto them, If ye think good, give me
> my price, and if not forbear.
>
> Zechariah 11:11–12

The poor of the flock understood what would happen. Jesus told his disciples that he was born to die and that he came, as Isaiah 53 proclaimed, to bear the iniquity of us all.

So what was he worth? The prophet asked, "What will you pay for the word of the Lord?"

> So they weighed for my price thirty pieces of silver. And
> the Lord said unto me, Cast it unto the potter: A goodly
> (paltry) price that I was priced at of them. And I took the
> thirty pieces of silver, and cast them to the potter in the
> house of the Lord. Then I cut asunder mine other staff,
> even Bands (Unity), that I might break the brotherhood
> between Judah and Israel.
>
> Zechariah 11:12–14

The insulting price of a slave, thirty pieces of silver, was how they valued beauty. So God told Zechariah to cast the money to the potter. Give it to the poor. Of course, this prophecy was exactingly fulfilled on that day two thousand years ago when Judas received the thirty pieces of silver from the evil shepherds of the nation, and then after realizing his error, cast it back to the priests in the Lord's house where the Bible then tells us that they unwittingly used the blood money to buy the worthless piece of land filled with potters shards in which to bury strangers.

Oh, how this story, which had just happened only a few days earlier, must have made the ears of those two men burn with awe and amazement when Jesus explained it to them on that wonderful walk on the road to Emmaus.

For further study:

1. From Zechariah 11:15-17 another shepherd is mentioned who is called foolish, he does not feed the flock but actually eats the flock and is given the name of the idol shepherd. Who is this shepherd?

2. Has God ever answered a prayer of yours because you insisted? Did it turn out for the best? What is a better way to pray?

3. What does it look like when God's will is written upon your heart?

PART 4

POEMS SINGING OF JESUS

WHY DO THE
HEATHEN RAGE?

THE SECOND PSALM sings of Jesus and his awesome reign as king over the earth. Yet shortly after our Lord's death and resurrection, Peter and John prayed to the Father quoting this psalm (Acts 4:24–28). Undoubtedly our Lord must have opened their eyes to its meaning, first on the road to Emmaus, and then later, during the forty days he spent with them prior to his ascension back to the Father.

> Why do the heathen rage, and the people imagine a vain thing? The kings of the earth set themselves, and the rulers take counsel together, against the Lord, and against his anointed, saying, Let us break their bands asunder and cast their cords from us.
>
> Psalm 2:1–3

In this dual prophecy of both the first and second comings of the Lord, the kings and rulers of the earth have and will say, "We will not have this man rule over us!"

Look at the Father's awesome reply.

> He that sitteth in the heavens shall laugh [he can't believe their audacity]: He shall have them in derision. Then shall he speak unto them in his wrath, and vex them in his sore displeasure. Yet have I set my king upon my holy hill of Zion. I will declare the decree: The Lord hath said unto me, Thou art my Son; this day I have begotten thee. Ask of me, and I shall give thee the heathen for thine inheritance, and the uttermost parts of the earth for thy possession. Thou shalt break them with a rod of iron; thou shalt dash them in pieces like a potter's vessel.
>
> Psalm 2:4–9

This is serious stuff! If I in my heart also say that I do not want Jesus to rule over me, I too will be broken.

Paul amplifies this prophecy with these words,

> Having made known unto us the mystery of his will...that... he might gather together in one all things in Christ, both which are in heaven, and which are on earth; even in him.
>
> Ephesians 1:9–10

Hinted at in Psalm 2 and revealed by Paul as the mystery of God's will, is that all, both Jews and Gentiles, earthly and heavenly kings and rulers, will be in Christ and under his lordship!

With that in mind, Psalm 2 ends with instructions to the wise.

> Be wise now therefore, O ye kings: Be instructed, ye judges of the earth. Serve the Lord with fear, and rejoice with trembling. Kiss the Son, lest he be angry, and ye perish from the way, when his wrath is kindled but a little. Blessed are all they that put their trust in him.
>
> Psalm 2:10–12

ON THE ROAD TO EMMAUS 289

Truly, our God is a consuming fire!

For further study:

1. What does "Kiss the Son, lest he be angry" mean to you? Do you think it could be associated with praise & worship?

2. "Ask of me, and I shall give thee the heathen for thine inheritance" has been used from many pulpits as a missionary verse. Do you feel that is the proper context of this verse?

3. Does Revelation 4:11 tie into the message of this psalm? What is the purpose of your existence according to Revelation 4:11?

THE SONG OF SONGS: THE SHEPHERD KING WITH HIS BRIDE

T HE SONG OF Solomon, written in the tenth century BC is the only one of a thousand and five songs penned by King Solomon, which God directed to be included into his Holy Word. To the unspiritual person, to the natural man, the Song of Songs is seen as an unattainable love manual for a husband and a wife to seek after, realizing that its perfection may not be reachable. Others, of simple intellect, see only an erotic oriental love poem in its verses. But we, three thousand years after its inspiration, can see the Song of Solomon in its proper light.

Scholars have concluded that there are two interpretive points of view. Portraits that are independent from each other but both correct nonetheless. First, the song is a divine picture of pure love.

Love without lust or austerity on the one hand and somberness on the other. It can be seen as God-ordained love, later called agape love in the New Testament, where the concept of self is lost in the presence of such a powerful force. It indeed can be seen as a goal for the God-ordained human marriage.

The second and more important interpretive point of view is that Solomon's Song of Songs is a wonderful and mystical love story between a shepherd king and his beautiful wife. We can see a powerful allegory and a prophetic picture of the ongoing marriage between the Son of Solomon, Jesus Christ the shepherd king, and his wife the church of Christ made up of both Jews and Gentiles as we consider the Song of Songs. So let's reflect upon this stunning poem, which sings of our Lord. It's not only a top-forty hit, but it's one of the greatest and most profound songs ever sung!

> Let him kiss me with the kisses of his mouth: For thy love
> is better than wine.
>
> The Song of Solomon 1:2

In the Bible, wine is synonymous with joy. We see in this verse that intimacy and joy are bed partners. Truly, intimacy with our husband is most joyous. As David proclaimed, "In thy presence is fullness of joy" (Psalm 16:11). For the Christian marriage today, this type of intimacy can only be attained as a couple focuses together upon Jesus.

> Because of the savor of thy good ointments thy name is as
> ointment poured forth, therefore do the virgins love thee.
>
> The Song of Solomon 1:3

Ointments were the medicines of the day. Of course, the Bible types oil as the Holy Spirit. Indeed our husband is spiritual health to our souls. Also, we see that the virgins, those people of purity, will be attracted to the Lord. They will love him.

> Draw me, we will run after thee.
>
> The Song of Solomon 1:4a

I can't reach my Lord on my own. I'm a sinner without the ability to find him. The Bible teaches that it's the Spirit who woos our hearts. Jesus told his disciples that they did not choose him, but it was he which chose them (John 15:16).

But look, after being drawn by him, then we can run after him. How good is that!

> I am black, but comely...as the tents of Kedar as the curtains of Solomon.
>
> The Song of Solomon 1:5

What a wonderful dichotomy. The bride recognizes that she is black like the tents of Kedar, that is, we understand our sin nature and of our need of repentance. But she also notes her comeliness. She grasps that she is white like the curtains of Solomon. Likewise, we comprehend that we have this wonderful treasure in earthen vessels. We revel in our knowledge that we have Christ in us, the hope of glory (Colossians 1:27)!

> Tell me, O thou whom my soul loveth, where thou feedest, where thou makest thy flock to rest at noon: For why should I be as one that turneth aside by the flocks of the companions?
>
> The Song of Solomon 1:7

Here we see that the king is also a shepherd. Of course, in this we see Jesus the good shepherd loud and clear. But also, isn't this so much like we are! The bride asks, "Where are you Lord? I don't want to hang out with the sheep I want to just be with you." Look at his answer.

> If thou know not, O thou fairest among women, go thy
> way forth by the footsteps of the flock, and feed thy kids
> beside the shepherds' tents.

> The Song of Solomon 1:8

"You will find me," the king replies, "when you travel with the flock." In other words, I'm in church. Look for me there along with other believers, and I will be found. And feed the kids. Take care of the little ones. I will be there too!

In verses 9–11, the king describes the beauty he sees in his bride. It's the comeliness that our husband see in us!

She responds,

> While the king sitteth at his table, my spikenard sendeth
> forth the smell thereof.

> The Song of Solomon 1:12

The king's table of course speaks to you and me of the table of the Lord. It reminds us of communion, of his sacrifice. And as the bride sits at that wonderful table, she takes on the sweet fragrance thereof!

> A bundle of myrrh is my well-beloved unto me; it shall lie
> all night betwixt my breasts.

> The Song of Solomon 1:13

Myrrh in the Bible always is seen in association with our Lord's sacrifice. Once again, this is the case here. How blessed is our Lord when we, like the bride, take to heart that sacrifice all night long!

> My beloved is unto me as a cluster of camphire in the
> vineyards of Engedi

> The Song of Solomon 1:14

Camphire (cypress trees) are cool and refreshing. Engedi is that wonderful oasis in the desert near the Dead Sea. The bride continues her response to her husband by noting that he is like an oasis in the desert. Likewise, our Lord is coolness and refreshment in this dry and dusty world we live in!

> Behold, thou art fair, my love; behold, thou art fair; thou hast doves eyes.
>
> The Song of Solomon 1:15

When the king twice says we are fair, he's not saying we are okay, that we are nice. No, in the Bible, to be fair means to be beautiful, to be ravishing! That's how our husband sees you and me! We are twice fair! Also, he notes that we have dove's eyes. The dove of course speaks of the Holy Spirit. Our groom sees his Spirit in my soul!

> I am the rose of Sharon, and the lily of the valleys.
>
> The Song of Solomon 2:1

The king brings beauty into my life! Not only is Jesus the bread of life, my sun and my shield, but he is the bright morning Star. He is the rose of Sharon and the lily of the valleys. Not only is he my provider and protector, he is most beautiful to behold!

> As the lily among thorns, so is my love among the daughters.
>
> The Song of Solomon 2:2

He sees me as a magnificent flower in the midst of this thorny world! I hope you are starting to take this in. He is not mad at you. He is not disappointed in you. He's madly in love with you and me. What a revelation! What a husband we have!

> As the apple tree among the trees of the wood, so is my beloved among the sons. I sat down under his shadow with great delight, and his fruit was sweet to my taste.
>
> The Song of Solomon 2:3

Oh, taste and see that the Lord is good! How wonderful it is to sit under the shadow of his wings. To be protected and provided for by our wonderful husband. Indeed, Jesus the Lord leaves me with a wonderful taste for more of him!

> He brought me to the banqueting house, and his banner over me was love.
>
> The Song of Solomon 2:4

Here I think of the wonderful banquet that we will partake of in that day not far away called the marriage feast of the lamb (Revelation 19:7). In that day, we will honeymoon, just as the bride in this song is doing. And his banner over us is love. We too have a banner now. We are Christian! We have Christ in us!

Next, after a night of love with our Lord, we enter a new day. Let's see how the bride takes on this fresh opportunity.

> The voice of my beloved! Behold, he cometh leaping upon the mountains, skipping upon the hills. My beloved is like a roe or a young hart: Behold, he standeth behind our wall, he looketh forth at the windows, showing himself through the lattice.
>
> The Song of Solomon 2:8–9

Now we see the king up and working. He is leaping and skipping over mountains and hills. We would say that he is taking on problems and challenges with ease and joy. But look, he is outside, separated a bit from his bride. He is on the other side of the wall, but he is showing himself through the window. Likewise, in our day today, this is how we see our king, how we see our husband. He is sort of veiled. He is a bit distant. Truly now we see but dimly. But in the future, we will see him face to face (1 Corinthians 13:12).

> My beloved spake, and said unto me, Rise up, my love, my fair one, and come away. For, lo, the winter is past, the rain

is over and gone; the flowers appear on the earth; the time of the singing of birds is come, and the voice of the turtle is heard in our land. The fig tree putteth forth her green figs, and the vines with the tender grape give a good smell. Arise, my love, my fair one, and come away.

The Song of Solomon 2:10–13

So picture this. The king is outside, working, while the bride is in her bed still, enjoying the afterglow of her night of love. But now her desire calls to her to join him in his business. The time is right. He says, "The fields are white for harvest. Let's not sleep away the day when we have so much to do." And then to accent his invitation, we see a reference to the fig tree and the vine. Both ripe with fruit and ready to be harvested. Of course, in Bible typology, these two plants always picture the nation of Israel. We in our day are living in the day this song is singing of. We today have seen Israel come back to life. Time is short, he would say to you and me. Let's go, bride. Let's go, church!

Take us the foxes, the little foxes that spoil the vines: For our vines have tender grapes.

The Song of Solomon 2:15

This is a warning from our friend. In the east, vineyards would be enclosed to keep out the spoilers. But little foxes could find openings in the rock walls and break in and eat the fruit. Here, we are reminded that we have an adversary who wants to break in and ruin us. He wants to see the fruit in our lives spoiled. The king is lovingly telling his bride to be on guard.

Unfortunately, like I can so often also do, in ignorance she misses the opportunity.

My beloved is mine, and I am his: He feedeth among the lilies. Until the day break, and the shadows flee away, turn, my beloved, and be thou like a roe or a young hart upon the mountains of Bether.

The Song of Solomon 2:16–17

You go ahead, my dear, is what she declares. I'm going to sleep in until the shadows flee away. It's ho-hum for the bride as it can be with me. I love you Lord, but I'm just too tired to meet with you this morning. You go on ahead. I'll catch up to you later.

Oh, how we can miss blessings he has for us when we don't answer his call. In this, I'm reminded of the proverb, "Those who seek me early shall find me" (Proverbs 8:17). As I respond to the Lord early in the day, early in a problem, early in life, I will find him in his promise!

> By night on my bed I sought him whom my soul loveth: I sought him but I found him not. I will rise now, and go about the city in the streets, and in the broad ways I will seek him whom my soul loveth:
>
> The Song of Solomon 3:1–2a

I like this. She missed the opportunity to be with her love, but as soon as she realized it, she went looking for him. This is great because we can do the same! And I'm glad for that. He's the lover of my soul. He tells me that as I draw near to him, he will draw near to me (James 4:8).

> I sought him, but I found him not.
>
> The Song of Solomon 3:2b

Sometimes, we don't find him immediately. He may delay a bit to draw out faith in my soul. I'm reminded of the story of Lazarus as I contemplate this principle. After Jesus learned that Lazarus was near death, we are told that he tarried for two days before going to Bethany to revive his friend. Dear reader, our wonderful husband's timing is always right on. If he hides a bit when we seek him, it will only hold a greater blessing when we see him revealed!

I found him who my soul loveth: I held him, and would not let him go, until I had brought him into my mother's house, and into the chamber of her that conceived me.

The Song of Solomon 3:4

Wow! I want to be like this wife! When she finds her man, she doesn't wait till Sunday to check him out in church. No, she meets him in intimacy in a near place. Right then and there! That's a good word for me also. When I find my love, I too, don't want to let him go!

So after a second night of love, we next see a beautiful morning procession revealing the king and his bride to others watching.

Who is this that cometh out of the wilderness like pillars of smoke, perfumed with myrrh and frankincense, with all powders of the merchant? Behold his bed, which is Solomon's; threescore valiant men are about it, of the valiant of Israel. They all hold swords, being expert in war: Every man hath a sword upon his thigh because of fear in the night.

The Song of Solomon 3:6–8

Others watching, picturing the people of the world, are asking, who is this woman being carried out of the desert smelling of myrrh and frankincense and being carried by a troop of majestic warriors? The answer of course is that she is the bride. She is the church of Christ made up of Jew and Gentiles who have embraced the shepherd king. Notice that she takes on the fragrance of her man (Myrrh, the sweet fragrance of Jesus' sacrifice, and frankincense, the aroma of a priest. These were both given to Jesus at the time of his birth.) and she is being brought out of a dry and dusty place escorted by men of war. These soldiers I believe can be seen as the angelic hosts, which the Bible assures are constantly ministering to us on an often unseen level in this dark world we inhabit.

> Go forth, O ye daughters of Zion, and behold King
> Solomon with the crown wherewith his mother crowned
> him in the day of his espousals, and in the day of the glad-
> ness of his heart.
>
> The Song of Solomon 3:11

"Check out the king. Look at the handsome man I love." These
are the words to the daughters of Zion who are watching. This is
my prayer too. Lord, help me to point people to you. You are the
one wearing the crown. You are the source of all joy and gladness.
Help me to show that to the daughters of Zion.

The next seven verses give a beautiful description of how
our husband views us. He describes his bride's beauty compara-
tively and in ways that can bring out much wonderful symbolism
toward how the Lord views his church. He concludes his praise
by saying, "Thou art all fair, my love; there is no spot in thee" (The
Song of Solomon 4:7). Indeed, only because of the remarkable
covering we as the bride have enjoyed can it be said that there is
no spot in us! Praise him for his wonderful gift!

> Come with me from Lebanon, my spouse, with me from
> Lebanon: Look from the top of Amana, from the top of
> Shenir and Hermon, from the lions dens, from the moun-
> tains of the leopards.
>
> The Song of Solomon 4:8

After the morning procession, the king once again invites his
bride to join him in the mountains. What a wonderful type! Here
we see Jesus, the husband of the second chance! Let's go, my love,
come with me as we go out and take on the many mountains and
difficulties in our world. Why would he want us to come with
him one could ask? He doesn't really need me.

> Thou hast ravished my heart, my sister, my spouse; thou
> hast ravished my heart with one of thine eyes, with one
> chain of they neck. How fair is thy love, my sister, my

spouse! How much better is thy love than wine! And the smell of thine ointments than all spices! Thy lips, O my spouse, drop as the honeycomb: Honey and milk are under thy tongue; and the smell of thy garments is like the smell of Lebanon. A garden enclosed is my sister, my spouse; a spring shut up, a fountain sealed.

The song of Solomon 4:9–12

Wow! This is too great to be true! The king is entirely taken back and taken away by the love he feels for his bride. He calls her his sister. This is so cool. In calling us his sister as well as his spouse, the king gives a fuller and deeper meaning to our relationship. Besides intimate lovers, we are best friends. Truly in Jesus, we have a friend like no other. A friend who is closer than a brother. We are the friends of God! So that's why he calls us to join him. Not because he needs us, but because he wants to be with us.

Look also how these verses end. The king proclaims that we are a beautiful enclosed garden. In the east, kings would have a private garden where they could retire and rest. Our king calls us his garden!

Let my beloved come into his garden, and eat his pleasant fruits.

The Song of Solomon 4:16

This is my prayer! The bride in humility, in respect, in love, recognizes that she is her love's fruitful garden. The Bible teaches that all things were created by him and for him, and for his pleasure, all things were made (Colossians 1:16). We are the garden of the Lord. And our fruit which he enjoys...why it's the fruit of the spirit! It's love, joy, peace, patience, kindness, gentleness, goodness, faith, meekness, and self-control (Galatians 5:22–23). It is righteousness, peace, and joy in the Holy Spirit (Romans 14:17). Dear believer, it is so important to bear fruit because we are his garden. He longs to enjoy the fruit we produce, and the wonderful thing about producing fruit is that it doesn't take any effort! The bud of the grape doesn't sweat it to bring forth that tasty delight; no, not at all. The only thing that bud does is to stay connected to the vine. That's it! Stay connected to the vine, dear bride!

> I am come into my garden, my sister, my spouse: I have gathered my myrrh, with my spice; I have eaten my honey-comb with my honey: I have drunk my wine with my milk: Eat, O friends; drink, yea, drink abundantly, O beloved.
>
> The Song of Solomon 5:1

Our king responds to our fruitful gift to him by thanking us for the myrrh and honey and wine we have offered back to him, and then he wonderfully invites others to share in the fruitfulness of our garden. Isn't this like it should be? The primary reason for the gifts of the Holy Spirit is not for our personal enjoyment and passion, but to be a witness to others of our redeemer. Jesus told his disciples that they would receive power from on high so they could be witnesses of the resurrection (Acts 1:8). When people see the fruit of love in my life, when I love others, his friends, then I am sharing my fruitful garden in the way God intended!

With the next verse, we start another wonder stanza of this beautiful song. Let's hear how it sounds!

> I sleep, but my heart waketh: It is the voice of my beloved that knocketh, saying, Open to me, my sister, my love, my dove, my undefiled: For my head is filled with dew, and my locks with the drops of the night.
>
> The Song of Solomon 5:2

In the east to this day, a man and a woman, a king and his queen, would not sleep together. Thus, we see the imagery of the king knocking upon the door (Revelation 3:20). He calls to his sister (friend), his love, his dove, his undefiled to let him come to her intimately. This time, it's in the middle of the night. And with this third invitation, we see something in our Lord. He isn't very predictable, is he? One time he will come in the morning, another in midday, and here it's in the middle of the night. Thus, it behooves me to always be listening for him. Let's see if the bride was.

> I have put off my coat; how shall I put it on? I have washed my feet; how shall I defile them?
>
> The Song of Solomon 5:3

Oh no, she's going to miss it again! This time though, it's not because of ignorance as the time previously, now we see her indifference. Dear husband, I'm in my nightgown. I'm comfortable and clean. I'm not really interested in your advances right now. I don't want to get dirty. Let's come together tomorrow is what she is basically saying. So off her man goes just as before! And that's the way of our Lord. He's constantly offering me invitations to share time with him. But he will not force himself upon me. He is the perfect gentleman. But he doesn't grovel and beg either. It's "see you later," if I pass on his offer to spend time with him!

A bit later, we see the woman regretting her missed opportunity to share love with her man.

> I opened to my beloved; but my beloved had withdrawn himself, and was gone: My soul failed when he spake: I sought him, but I could not find him.
>
> The Song of Solomon 5:6

As she (we) realized she had failed when he spake, she did the right thing. We can do the right thing also. She sought him. She looked for him!

In the city, the bride asked the daughters of Jerusalem if they had seen her beloved. Tell him I am sick with love if you see him, is what she said. In response, they ask her what's so special about her husband that she would be so upset in not being able to immediately find him.

Here is her wonderful reply of his beauty. Here is how our Jesus will appear when we too find him on that wonderful day not far away!

> My beloved is white and ruddy [God is light, and God is love], the chiefest among ten thousand. His head is of most fine gold [speaking of his divinity], his locks are bushy, and black as a raven [he does not change; he does not grow old]. His eyes are as the eyes of doves by the rivers of waters [he has spiritual eyes], washed with milk, and fitly set. His cheeks are as a bed of spices, as sweet flowers [he smells great]: His lips like lilies, dropping sweet smelling myrrh. His hands are as gold rings set with beryl [he has authority]: His belly is as bright ivory overlaid with sapphires. His legs are as pillars of marble, set upon sockets of fine gold [his walk is with certainty] His countenance is as Lebanon, excellent as the cedars. His mouth is most sweet: Yea, he is altogether lovely. This is my beloved, and this is my friend, O daughters of Jerusalem.
>
> The Song of Solomon 5:10–16

O Lord, you are altogether lovely, and you are our friend. Give us eyes to see you like this!

> Wither is thy beloved gone, O fairest among women? Wither is thy beloved turned aside? That we may seek him with thee
>
> The Song of Solomon 6:1

Look what the bride's praises did. The daughters of Jerusalem wanted to see him also. That's what happens when I speak of his beauty and majesty. Others will be motivated to seek him with me!

> My beloved is gone down into his garden, to the beds of spices, to feed in the garden, and to gather lilies.
>
> The Song of Solomon 6:2

As she praises him, she realizes where he is! As we praise him, we too will find him. Jesus told his disciples that God seeks those who will worship him in spirit and in truth (John 4:23).

In finding her beloved, he responded with praises of her beauty and then gave a wonderful and powerful description of the church, which the bride depicts.

> There are threescore queens and fourscore concubines, and virgins without number [the church is made up of different categories of women, if you will, some seemingly of higher estate than others]. My dove, my undefiled is but one; she is the only one of her mother.
>
> The Song of Solomon 6:8–9

Just like God is a compound unity, so is the church. Father, Son, and Spirit, queens, concubines, and virgins.

Next, look at the qualities he sees in her. Consider the qualities that we as the church possess.

> Who is she that looketh forth as the morning [she has perspective], fair as the moon [she reflects his glory], clear as the sun [she is empowered by his Spirit], and terrible as an army with banners [she can take on the enemy]?
>
> The Song of Solomon 6:10

The answer of course, is it's you and me. It's the church of Christ.

Her husband goes on to say of his bride,

> How beautiful are thy feet [In describing the armor of God, Paul states that our feet are shod with the gospel of peace (Ephesians 6:15). He also proclaims, "How beautiful are the feet of them that preach the gospel of peace" (Romans 10:15.)] thy navel is round like a goblet, which wanteth not liquor [he sees us as independent from the world],...thy stature is like a palm tree, I will take hold

of the boughs thereof [Like a palm tree, we become more fruitful as we age and mature].

The Song of Solomon 7:1–2, 8

As she takes in his praises, as she considers his words to her, something wonderful happens.

Come my beloved, let us go forth into the field: Let us lodge in the villages. Let us get up early to the vineyards; let us see if the vine flourish, whether the tender grape appear, and the pomegranates bud forth:

The Song of Solomon 7:11–12

Realizing that her husband has work to do, the bride desires to join him. No longer missing her husband's request for intimacy and togetherness, here in her maturity, she actually makes the first move! I like that!

Finally, in chapter 8, we come to the close of this wonderful love story. We read (verse 1) of the bride longing to kiss her husband no matter where they might travel (in that culture, it was and is taboo to kiss your wife in public). She asked him to set a seal upon her heart (verse 6) which would help her through the difficult times ahead (the seal of course is a type of the Holy Spirit with which we are sealed). She noted that love cannot be purchased in verse 7 (salvation is not of works), and she was concerned about her little sister (young believers) in verse 8. In ending this wonderful love story, the bride makes a request, which will come up again and again as we read God's Word, "Come quickly, Lord!"

Make haste, my beloved, and be thou like to a roe or to a young hart upon the mountains of spices.

The Song of Solomon 8:14

And the Spirit and the bride say, Come. And let him that heareth say, Come. And let him that is athirst come. And whosoever will, let him take the water of life freely...He which testifieth these things saith, Surely I come quickly. Amen. Even so, come, Lord Jesus.

Revelation 22:17 and 20

The grace of our Lord Jesus Christ be with you all. Amen

Revelation 22:21

There we have Solomon's Song of Songs. The true love story for the ages! No, it's not just a romantic and erotic Oriental love story, but it truly is a song of Jesus' love for you and me. I'm so thankful to my husband that he calls me his bride. He calls you that too!

Lastly, in considering the possibly unsettling idea that we are all called his bride, we should end with that most famous quote from A. W. Tozer, "An infinite God can give all of himself to each of his children as if none other existed."

For further study:

1. From Solomon's Song 1:7 the bride asks her man where he is. He told her in verse 8 to hang out with the flocks and she would find him. How does this translate to you today when you want to meet with Jesus?

2. What happened after the bride decided to sleep-in and decline her love's invitation to join him? (See Song of Solomon 3:1-2) Has that ever happened to you?

3. Do you believe that the Lord is ravished by you as the Song of Solomon 4:9-12 sings? Why is this so?

4. The Song of Solomon 4:16 states we are our beloved's fruit bearing garden. Can you think of a time in your life when Jesus would not want to spend time in his garden? What was happening during those times?

5. According to Solomon's Song 6:1-2, what are two benefits of praising the Lord?

Epilogue

So there we have it! On the road to Emmaus, Jesus explained to those two privileged men all of the things speaking of him in the law and the prophets. Obviously, in this little book, I have only scratched the surface of this wonderful topic, but my prayer for you is that this book has warmed your heart as you consider and see the Old Testament in a bigger and more liberating way. I hope I have stimulated many of you to search the scriptures to see that indeed, they testify of him (John 5:39).